A MORAL RESPONSE TO INDUSTRIALISM

The Lectures of Reverend Cook
in Lynn, Massachusetts

JOHN TAYLOR CUMBLER
University of Louisville

State University of New York Press
ALBANY

Published by
State University of New York Press, Albany

© *1982 State University of New York*

All rights reserved

Printed in the United States of America

For information, address State University of New York
Press, State University Plaza, Albany, N.Y., 12246

Library of Congress Cataloging in Publication Data
Cumbler, John T.
A Moral Response to Industrialism
(SUNY series on American social history)
Bibliography: p.
1. Lynn (Mass.)—Social conditions—Addresses,
essays, lectures. 2. Lynn (Mass.)—Industries—
History—Addresses, essays, lectures. 3. Cook,
Joseph, 1838-1901. I. Title. II. Series
HN80.L97C85   974.4'5   81-9338
ISBN 0-87395-558-7   AACR2
ISBN 0-87395-559-5 (pbk.)

A MORAL RESPONSE
TO INDUSTRIALISM

SUNY Series on American Social History
Elizabeth Pleck and Charles Stephenson, Editors

Contents

Acknowledgments

This work owes much not only to the Reverend Joseph Cook and the characters in Lynn, Massachusetts, who crowded into that city's largest lecture hall to applaud, cheer, and hiss, but also to my friends and colleagues who have helped me bring the Reverend Mr. Cook and his friends, colleagues and detractors to the attention of the modern reader. Professor Mary Hawkesworth and Professor Bonnie Blustein helped much with this introduction. Professor Blustein helped me in the initial drafts of the introduction, especially with her knowledge of "the Mc-Kleans Asylume." Professor Hawkesworth read and reread several drafts of the introduction and the various notes clarifying my thoughts and working on the arguments. Professor Lew Erenberg was very helpful both in giving me criticism and in directing me to important sources of which I was unaware. Professor Milton Cantor not only spent an afternoon helping me work out some of the ideas, but also gave considerable time in reading and helping me with the manuscript itself. Kathy Shortridge's critical reading of the manuscript in its early stages helped both the style of the work and its contents. Professor William Morison not only shared with me material on Joseph Cook, but also enlightened me on Cook's theological role in late-nineteenth-century religious circles. Professor Ray Shortridge, Judith Cumbler, Rita Jones, Beverly Morris, Charles Stephenson, Lee Shai Weissbach, Sharon Mills, and Janet Batik all helped get this work beyond rough drafts into final form. Although he did not directly contribute to the completion of this work, Professor Sam Warner's training and friendship has always been a factor in the best of my work. My family, Judith, Ethan, and Kazia, has been helpful especially in keeping me going.

1

The Setting and the Man

In 1871 America had finished burying her dead and honoring her returning veterans. Farmers and laborers, merchants and millers, seamstresses and entrepreneurs returned to the peacetime occupations once held by their fathers and mothers. Yet the society to which they returned had changed dramatically. The war had settled the great moral issue of the antebellum period, slavery. But changes in the process of production had already begun to crystallize the issue that would dominate Americans' lives throughout the remainder of the century, industrialization. Cities, which had been growing rapidly since the early part of the century, now reached a size and complexity that confronted the citizen of the time with a strange and different phenomenon. The inherited institutions of small-town and rural America seemed strangely out of step with the new urban and industrial society.

In Massachusetts, a state with a large industrial base and a high level of urbanization, the question how best to deal with the needs of individuals in a changing society was raised by the leaders of the Congregational churches. With the rapid decline in rural and small-town populations, Congregationalists became increasingly aware of the falling rate of church attendance. For this reason, a Committee on Home Evangelization headed by Daniel Noyes, Secretary of the Home Missionary Society, was formed in 1865 to investigate the steady decline in church membership. The committee reported that the growing divisions between rich and poor, especially in the urban churches, was cutting down on attendance. They recommended that the church seek ways to overcome such divisions and that the church attempt to reach out to the

1

poor. Few churches responded immediately to the report. But in 1871, a young Congregational minister in Lynn, the Reverend Joseph Cook, whose church had burned down and who was forced temporarily to hold Sunday evening services in the city's newly built Music Hall, decided to use the opportunity provided by the new, larger location to hold services that focused upon the issues raised by the committee. Since Lynn was a factory town and most of its residents were factory workers, Cook delivered a series of lectures on the topic of factory reform. The lectures proved to be an unparalleled success. Not only did Cook interest his own congregation, but his flamboyant style and charges against certain manufacturers of corruption, vice, and immorality brought out the community in numbers unequaled in the city's history.

The lectures were a success in part because Cook was a master of the art of dramatic lecture. He knew when to titillate his audiences with suggestions of immorality and vice, and when to appear the embattled crusader. Yet, the Reverend Mr. Cook was also a success because, as an articulate spokesperson for the troubled middle class in the industrializing Northeast, he called attention to the tremendous changes occurring in the world. "The new star of the steam engine blazed across the mechanical sky; took a fixed place in it; and immediately there was a new grouping of constellations. The vast manufacturing establishments which existed at a distance from towns were transferred to crowded populations."[1] The new constellations to which he referred were the products of a social reordering caused by industrialization. With its factory machine production, divided and specialized labor tasks, aggregation of capital, creation of "armies of workers," rapid increase in size of cities, and advancing technologies, industrialization forced Americans to come to terms with a totally new complexity of experience. It provided the opportunity for great economic achievements and indeed, for liberating people from grinding poverty and labor. However, it also produced poverty, insecurity at the margins of survival, and overcrowded slum conditions for thousands of workers. For manufacturers, it meant unparalleled wealth and opulence, for urban dwellers, an influx of new and often alien populations, and for intellectuals, "an immense amount of material," observed John Dewey, "foreign to and often times inconsistent with the most prized intellectual heritage of the western world."[2]

Industrialization proceeded at different rates in different regions and had varying impacts on various sectors of the population. It was in rural New England that Americans first experienced the traumas of industrialization, and the ideas that developed there tended to set the pattern for the rest of the nation.[3] It was here, with the Waltham and Lowell systems, that the integrated factory system in textile production first appeared. (Lowell, discussed in more detail in Appendix A, was also unusually innovative in the antebellum period in other than its early factory structure. Lowell, and later Lawrence, were known for a system of controlled boardinghouses that sheltered the eulogized "Lowell Girls."[4] The image of these female textile operatives who worked during the day and wrote poetry at night afforded Lowell an exceptional status in the nation's mind.)

During the period immediately following the Civil War, Americans began to realize that industrialization and factory regimentation constituted the wave of the future for most cities. This realization dawned first upon the New Englanders, who led the nation in industrial development.

Despite major innovations in technology and production, which had occurred in the 1850s and which had found widespread application the war itself (particularly standardized mass-produced clothing), as late as 1869 most production outside of New England was still powered by muscle or water, rather than by steam.[5] In that year, the average number of wage earners was only 8.15 per establishment, and most were shops still based upon family and partnership. Although at the close of hostilities the nation as a whole was just beginning its rapid industrial development, New England (particularly Massachusetts) was already well on the way. Massachusetts had twice the number of factory hands as Ohio, and its investment per manufacturing establishment was twice the national average. Massachusetts led in number of shoe workers, and the shoe industry was third on the list of industries in value added.[6]

In Lynn, Massachusetts, a "shoe town," industrialization began early; within a generation it substantially altered that community. Coming to the shoe industry between 1855 and 1865, industrialization brought to Lynn most of the characteristics that we have come to identify with it: the factory system, mechanization, steam power, the division of labor, and a flood of unskilled laborers. The rapidity and extent of change created anxiety and concern among several sectors of the community. Few people were indifferent to the change and most were militant in expressing their feelings about it.

INDUSTRIAL CHANGE IN LYNN

The change in shoe production began slowly and within a framework that did not appear to radically alter the existing society. Shoe production in the early nineteenth century occurred within the small shoe shops, which, in the case of Lynn, came to dominate the city. Within these shops, master workmen, journeymen, and apprentices produced shoes either for local customers or for merchants who sold them to a larger market. There was no great social or spatial distance between those involved in production and those involved in selling. Masters and journeymen alike saw themselves as producers of wealth and as pillars of their society. Although there were divisions and cleavages within that society, the community seemed inclusive to most of its members. It was a coherent collectivity in which individuals appeared to be in control of their own lives and work. As the markets for finished shoes expanded into the South and the Caribbean, merchants became more involved in bulk ordering from the shoe shops to sell to these new markets. Consequently, the production process was slowly reorganized. Taking advantage of the surplus labor of the New England countryside, the larger merchants and manufacturers began to divide up the labor process and "put out" (send out) cut leather uppers to be "bound" (sewn together) by women in the region's rural and seacoast areas. Even in the old shoe shops, wives and daughters had often performed the tasks of binding. However, when Lynn merchants and larger manufacturers began reorganizing shoemaking in order to penetrate new markets, larger and larger batches of binding were contracted out. Upon completion, these were returned to the city and shipped to journeymen, who would "last" (sew) them to the soles. Access to capital, facilitated by the development of Lynn's banking system and the successful expansion into new markets, encouraged the city's manufacturers to increase their scale of operations; they hired master workmen who specialized in cutting leather* in the large factories, put out the cut uppers for binding, and had the uppers lasted by skilled journeymen. Thus, these divisions of labor and of the factory system increased complexity of organization as well as production and profits. Fewer and fewer of the shoes produced in Lynn came from the shops of the independent master workmen with their small crews of journeymen

*Cutting leather was an important task because it involved not only judging the quality of the leather involved but also getting the most possible cuts from the irregularly shaped leather. Since leather was a major cost item, a good cutter could make the difference between profit and loss.

and apprentices; rather, the shoes increasingly came from the factories with groups of skilled workers. Yet even this major change in the production process did not radically alter the city. The old independent cordwainers and their small "ten-footers," as the shops were called, were still familiar sights. Even those skilled workers who were employed by the large manufacturers continued to identify with the tradition of the independent producer. They contiuned to have a "producer ideology" and to accept labor theory of value: that a product is given its value by the labor embodied in it. Lynn's merchants and professionals felt comfortable with the new developments, for they added to the city's wealth without radically changing the structure and appearance of the old community. Also, of course, the new manufacturers could point with pride to their new homes as well as factories and pronounce them the products of hard work and initiative, of major benefits to the whole community.

The manufacturers' increased wealth and new form of organization allowed them to take advantage of a technological breakthrough in the sewing machine. The sewing machine, initially powered by foot, was quickly adapted to steam-driven belts, which enabled a single worker to bind several more shoes in the same period of time. Beginning in 1855, a growing number of manufacturers began utilizing sewing machines and eventually moved to larger factories, where they could link up those machines to steam power. As the manufacturers turned to mechanized production, more and more unskilled workers, particularly women, came to the factories to do their binding not by hand but by machine.

After the introduction of the sewing machine, demand for "heeled shoes" increased, and large numbers of journeymen were also brought into the expanded factories to "heel" shoes. The manufacturers, increasingly concerned over the cost of labor, encouraged further segmentation in the labor processes so that more could be done by cheap, unskilled operatives, freeing the more expensive skilled labor for the most difficult jobs. In 1862 another technological innovation changed the shoe business: the introduction of the McKay stitching machine, which could stitch directly through the inner sole, upper, and outer sole. This allowed the production of eighty pairs of shoes an hour, whereas the manual method could produce only one pair; moreover, the McKay stitcher required less skill to operate. By demonstrating the successful use of steam, the McKay stitcher also provided the impetus for a dozen other innovations which divided the making of shoes into over two dozen tasks performed by a series of machines as a substitute for what the old cordwainers had done by hand. The operators for these machines were recruited from the old shoe shops, the surrounding countryside, and communities of the foreign-born in neighboring Boston. With the introduction of machines in the 1860s, the *Lynn Recorder* noted, "operatives are pouring in as fast as room can be made for them, buildings for shoe factories are going up in every direction," and "the hum of machinery is heard on every hand."[7]

In 1880 an old cordwainer, David Johnson, who had "spent [his] early days in the old-time shoemaker's shop," wrote a history of Lynn. Though lamenting the loss of the old-time shoemakers, who had given to the "gentle craft of St. Crispin" its romantic nature, he was also impressed with the wealth and progress that seemed to come with the introduction of machinery. The new age amazed Johnson and his peers, for they had "seen the unlimitable power of steam in its ten thousand applications to the wants of business and the comfort of mankind, spread all over the civilized world, revolutionizing commerce and every branch of manufacture. . . . Every day brings rumors of new wonders, and the end is not yet."[8] And for Johnson the adoption of these wonders was leading to the perfection of the shoemaking. "The work done in Lynn, in every branch of the shoe business, was never so good as at present. The law of adaptation is recognized, and guides every process. There is little waste, and that little is becoming less. Everything is utilized. In short, scientific exactness takes the place of guess-work and systematic economy, the place of wasteful methods."[9] Indeed, for Johnson the revolution in shoe production was clearly linked to the "high quality"[10] of Lynn's residents and their willingness to move forward with all the progressive images and rhetoric of the day—science, innovation, hard work, and excellence.

Johnson's history of Lynn, summarized in the following paragraph, transmits a sense of his belief in the future:

> Capital was attracted to it, and the inventive genius of our people and the skill of our mechanics, developed its resources and improved the quality of its products. The enterprise and intelligence of our merchants availed themselves to every invention and applicance designed to improve the product or to cheapen its cost; and today, as the result of long years of patient toil, of ingenious contrivance, and of business enterprise, the manufacturers of Lynn are able to offer to the world of buyers the advantages of the highest excellence that has been reached in this department of human industry.[11]

Johnson's book, with its nostalgia for the past, yet optimism for the future, is the history of one who left the shops and looked to the growth

of abstractions, not people. The benefits flowing from all this industry
and toil accrue to the buyers—as he saw it—but in reality, the manufacturers were the principal beneficiaries. For the shoemakers who tried to
remain in the old independent patterns, and for those others who
found their livelihood not in the old cordwainer's shop but sitting at a
factory bench or tending a machine for a wage, the reality was not as
pleasant. The old concept of independence—so important to the producer ideology—was gone. The discipline of low wages, autocratic
employers, and economic insecurity dictated life. Although Lynn merchants availed themselves of every invention to cheapen the production
costs, the results for the worker were wage reductions and increasing
subdivisions of the labor process. And although merchants began their
activity in hopes of tapping expanding markets, the reorganiztion of
the production process soon allowed Lynn manufacturers to produce
far more shoes than the market could bear. This process did not lead to
reduced production, but to a scramble for greater efficiency and lower
production costs, which in turn led to a continued crisis in the shoe
industry, which was continually plagued with boom–bust cycles and
flooded markets. The manufacturers with greater resources could
weather these crises by laying off workers, decreasing production, and
reducing wages. But for those caught at the bottom of the economic
system, those who worked the machines, who came "pouring in as fast
as room. . . . [could] be made for them,"[12] only to find that very little
room indeed was made, the crises meant unemployment, short wages,
cutbacks in necessities, doubling up with friends and relatives, or moving on to explore some other possibility; in other words, they meant
insecurity.

Johnson was right in emphasizing progress: the revolution in the
shoe industry did bring new wealth and prosperity to Lynn. For although the old artisan cordwainers had had a strong sense of pride in
their productive role, their lives had been quite meager. The ten-
footers with all their comraderie were also small and cramped, hot in
the summer, cold in the winter. The homes of most artisans were small
and sparsely furnished; indeed, one would be hard pressed to argue
that they were better than the homes that skilled shoe workers occupied
later. Yet the old artisan did enjoy a certain security, which the factory
worker, no matter how skilled, did not possess. He made shoes on
demand. The older technology also limited the number of shoes produced and, except during major collapses in the economy, shoe
workers did not tend to turn out more shoes than the demand war-
ranted. This was not the case after the introduction of mechanized
factory production.

Although markets originally were the stimulus to expansion, technology and industrialization themselves became propelling forces, which drove merchants and manufacturers beyond existing markets in an attempt to maintain competitiveness. Competition dictated technological innovation, which in turn dictated greater production, which then generated more innovation and still greater production. This production vastly outstripped demand for shoes, creating crises in the industry with resulting depressions, layoffs, wage cuts and general economic insecurity for the employees. The structure of the lending institutions, which offered credit to manufacturers on the basis of size, enabled the larger manufacturers to weather these periodic crises far more successfully than small artisans or wage workers.

Thus the demand for technological advance and even larger-scale production propelled Lynn's industrialization onward. With each recession the city's manufacturers saw that only large efficient factories weathered the difficult times. For this reason, profits were reinvested in more machinery and expansion. As the factories grew in size and scale, so did the number of workers dependent upon wages for their livelihood. Many of these workers were former artisans and journeymen who had apprenticed in the old ten-footers. For these workers the new factories meant unceasing din, increased regimentation, and loss of independence and status. They were no longer artisans but employees, dependent upon their employer and his success, which often entailed periodic wage cuts and layoffs. Thus they were caught in the contradiction of being dependent for employment upon a capitalist's success, while that success depended upon their own exploitation as workers. Shaped in the image of the independent artisan and the labor theory of value, they sought to come to terms with their new position and their loss of status. They looked for explanation to various movements and social theories, some of which were progressive, others nostalgic and romantic, and all a response to new social conditions.

But old artisans were not the only ones drawn into the expanding factories. Others, with fewer skills and resources, also came. Women from both the city and surrounding countryside were quickly recruited. Many daughters and wives of shoe workers, who had traditionally worked as binders, continued in that trade as the sewing machine came into widespread use. With the adaptation of the sewing machine to steam power these women left their homes for the large factories being built in downtown Lynn. They often worked in the same building with their parents, older siblings, or other relatives; often they returned home for meals. For them, the move from home to factory, although dramatic, was cushioned by the fact that they were making the move within the context of the family environment. The women of Lynn were joined in the factories by others who left the farms of New England for work in the city. Still others, including many of Irish descent, came from Boston in search of employment. These women lived in boarding houses or with local families.

Like the male operatives, these women faced insecurity—low wages, layoffs, and underemployment. For those with families, there was the possibility of a collective cushion between themselves and the harsh consequences of unemployment. Those without families had fewer resources in coping with such problems, yet even for them the factories offered something that was not available at home: a potential for employment, for a husband, or perhaps for freedom from the stifling confines of a small rural community characterized by limited opportunity and a declining male population. Despite the drawbacks of factory work—regimentation, arbitrary authority, noise, constraints on movement, lack of control over work—that constituted factories virtual prisons, they were prisons that paid wages, however, meager.

Women were not the only new workers to be drawn into Lynn's factories. With the subdivision of labor, increased mechanization, and expansion of the factory system, thousands of male as well as female workers flooded the city. Many of them had limited skills and were dependent for a livelihood upon the expanded demand for unskilled labor. Those without families crowded into boardinghouses or lived with other workers who took in boarders to help make ends meet. They were paid the lowest possible rates and could seldom save enough to get through hard times or seasonal layoffs, which occurred twice in a year in the Lynn factories. They were forced during these intervals to look elsewhere for work, either in construction or in other occupations. Most of them were young and without strong family ties in Lynn. They included farmhands from New Hampshire, Vermont, and Western Massachusetts, the children of Boston laborers and immigrants, and immigrants and their offspring from Ireland and Canada.

In the early morning hours, Lynn's streets, torn up with new construction, were filled with a sound unknown in the days when the ten-footers dominated the landscape. Thousands of people spilled out of the boardinghouses and homes clustered around Lynn and moved as a disciplined mass to the factory buildings of the central district. For old-time residents, familiar with large aggregates of people only during the recent Civil War, this mass resembled an army. It was an army of individuals regimented by the machine, the clock on the factory wall, the authority of the new master sergeant: the shop foreman. For those accustomed to the small informal workshops of the "gentle craft of St. Crispin," this new army of toilers was both exciting and frightening: exciting in its potential to create wealth, frightening in its newness and its challenge to their position in a rapidly changing world.[13]

Lynn's army of industrial workers was especially alarming because in 1860 Lynn had been the scene of the nation's largest strike. At that time the factory system was just being introduced to the city, wages were low, unemployment was high, and the shoe workers went out into the streets demanding higher wages and greater control over their jobs. Almost once a week a procession with over a thousand marchers passed through the streets. The largest demonstration, with more than six thousand workers waving banners and chanting slogans of solidarity, stunned the city. Women shoe workers were very much in evidence. They adopted the slogan, "American Ladies Will Not Be Slaves: Give Us a Fair Compensation and We Labour Cheerfully," and were conspicuously active in the 1860 strike activity. At a time when the ideal of womanhood was defined by Victorian notions of submissive deference to the male world and when acceptable female activity consisted exclusively of church work and social clubs, Lynn's working women came forward as independent actors on the economic stage. Their activities implied refusal to be "slaves" not only to the manufacturers but to male dominance generally; they challenged not only factory owners but also the middle class, with its Victorian image of fragile passive womanhood.

Lynn's nonworking classes were assured by the strikers that the peaceful walkout represented no threat to the standing order. One worker wrote in a song about the strike that the workers "need no rifles to keep them at peace: By the right of our cause we shall win: But no rum, and no outside police."[14] Although the song insisted on the pacific nature of the walkout, it touched upon two issues that came to dominate the strike and later clashes between labor and capital: the issues of social order and the police and moral reform. The strikers of 1860 perceived no need for outside police because they did not feel that they were an unruly, uncontrollable mob, but self-disciplined protestors, capable of policing themselves whether in the streets or in their private lives: witness their commitment to "no rum." However, to the manufacturing elite, Lynn's strikers did not appear so peaceable. During the height of the walkout, when strikers attempted to prevent the product of scab work from leaving town, the local marshal became involved in a scuffle with strikers. His failure to overpower the strikers convinced manufacturers that an insurrectionary crowd was trying to seize control of the city, and they prevailed upon the mayor to call out the state militia as well as police from several surrounding communities. Their presence heightened tension and created several disturbances. The strike ended after two months, but the manufacturers would not sign a formal notice of wages presented by the strikers, thereby refusing to reconize their new collective identity; however, several manufacturers did increase wages.[15]

More important, perhaps, than resolution of the strike were the images it created. For labor, the strike was a newfound demonstration of the power and potential of collective action. For manufacturers, it indicated a need for more control and order in the city. For the middle class, it represented a specter of disorder, a threat to their treasured image of a cohesive community.

The strike of 1860 not only marked a watershed between old and new productive systems, but it also catalyzed issues that would dominate Lynn as it attempted to cope with the mid-century's rapid changes. Such issues would occur later in other towns and industries across the nation. They gave focus to the question of working women and to the contradiction between the reality of their position and the widespread cult of "true womanhood." Workers also faced the contradiction between the old individualistic values, including such themes as equality and the labor theory of value, and new exercises in collective action and experiences of collective identity. Finally, the strike challenged the idea of community cohesion: manufacturers demanded order and repression, and labor called upon the community for support against outside intervention.

For the middle class, the 1860 strike represented a fearful specter. Collective action threatened romanticized notions about independent individual actions as the basis of the common good. The dearly held ideals of the transcendentalists and antebellum romantics were rooted in the conception of society as composed of independent actors sharing a vision of the common good.[16] This strike presented them with the image of a class-ridden society rife with irreconcilable differences and informed by opposing definitions of the good. It was a conflict that left no room for the independent viewpoint or the neutral middle ground. Both workers and manufacturers demanded that the middle class take sides and the resulting class alignments shook the middle-class world. In many ways the strike prefigured the Civil War itself: the romantic individual, the solitary moralist, was overwhelmed by a demand for mass action to defend moral principle. Slavery had been the major moral issue of the New England transcendentalists and social reformers; yet resolution of that issue required a denial of the very individualism that had been the basis for their moral system.[17] The Civil War was a cataclysmic event, which shattered middle-class illusions and prompted a search for a new moral position, a new system of order, a new concept of the moral community. And that community had to exist in a real community increasingly divided between worker and manufacturer, whose class division resembled at times in its intensity the wartime sectional divisions of North and South. It was within such a community that the Reverend Joseph Cook came to Lynn, a man trained in the traditions of the old moral order, searching for a new one amidst chaos and conflict.

THE REVEREND JOSEPH COOK

Joesph Cook, christened Flavius Josephus Cook, was born in 1838 in Ticonderoga, New York, of an old New England farm family, that had migrated to the region at the end of the eighteenth century. He came to Lynn in 1870 as acting minister of the First Congregational Church and soon became the leading spokesman for the city's middle class. It was a most appropriate role, for Cook's own life reflected many of the conflicts that then absorbed the middle class. His training and background enabled Cook to offer a solution to this class, specifically, moral reform. Accepting the hierarchical structure of society, Cook's moral reform would be guided by social reformers acting through the churches and schools to create a new moral order for society. Ultimately, this solution could not resolve the basic problems that confronted a nation then hurling itself into industrialization. It looked back upon a romantic ideal that could never again be resurrected. Neither the workers nor the entreprenurial class would accept such a solution, and without their acceptance it was hollow. Notwithstanding Cook's failure, his moral reform foreshadowed the traditional middle-class response to rapid industrialization and class division.

William Cook, Flavius's father, wished his only child educated in the best possible schools. Notwithstanding the financial burden, Flavius, at the age of thirteen, was sent to Vowton Academy, then Whitehall, and later to Phillips, Andover, "in order to be a success in life and influence events." William Cook was a strong force in his son's life and kept in constant contact, mostly through letters focusing upon affairs of the farm, the nation, and his son's character. Like many early-nineteenth-century farmers, he was concerned about a number of social and moral issues of the day. Thus, he was active in the formation of the Republican party, and strongly opposed to the expansion of slavery. "I don't wish to meddle with slavery where it has a right to exist, where it is constitutional, but I will do all in my power to stop the extension of the great evil."[18] Furthermore, although William Cook raised race horses, he opposed gambling. In addition, he was strongly opposed to drinking[19] and other unspecified sins. Although he did not want Flavius Cook to abandon studies for social causes, he hoped that his son would be concerned about contemporary social issues and would eventually follow in the tradition of transcendental individualism and become a major influence in the world. "Whenever you can see or hear of ones taking the lead, advancing new thoughts, new ideas, and new things, you will find the world's people to follow him. . . . Therefore it stands you in hand to try and take the lead and strive to be the one that is looked up to for new things, new thoughts, new ideas."[18] To that end William Cook urged his son to be prepared. "As you seem to think that your mission is to do good here in this world of ignorance, sin and vanity, it is necessary that you should be thoroughly educated."[20]

Nonetheless, his practical sense demanded that Flavius Cook keep his reforming zeal within sensible bounds. "Don't follow after any of the 'isms' of the day for they are productive of no good." And like many fathers, William Cook was concerned that his son not let his interest in social issues interrupt his studies. "I could say much as regards your course and pursuit of doing good to the world's teeming masses. . . . Remember that you are but a boy yet and not sufficiently experienced in these things to reform the world." He went on to remind his son what parents have reminded their children for ages: "Let others step in and do this business [of doing good] now as you have done your share. I see by your last letter that you pay three times the attention to other business that you do to your class studies. This I think is sorry. *Your class studies are what cost you money.* Other things can be attended to at a less expense."[21]

The Cooks were farmers, and William Cook wanted to give his son an education that would enable him to become an important figure in society, as well as to cultivate an awareness of the sacrifices needed to be a farmer. His letters constantly emphasized the difference between the hard work of a farmer and the easy life of the son: "The prospect is not very favorable for the farmer. Wool is low, provisions is high . . . You must be prudent of your money . . . Can't you get into some business so as to pay your way? It is hard for me to have to borrow the money for to keep you along."[22] His view of the world was dominated by a reality which continuously faced the farmers of the nineteenth century and drove thousands from the land. "Things look gloomy and desolate," he complained; "the prospects are very slim for the farms."[23] Indeed, the father made it very clear that life was better for those who did not till the earth for a living: "You think you are fitted to take things easy and pleasantly by their smooth handle. Was there ever any other handle presented to you, but the smooth handle. You have gone through life as it were in a cushioned rocking chair bolsterd up as it were with downy pillow and drawn by a good team. All you have to do is ask and it is given. You should think of these things for the time is coming when you will not be thus provided for. . . . "[24]

William Cook constantly reminded his son of the importance of independence, so essential to the rural ideology. "Learn to paddle your own canoe," he asserted—by which he meant financial as well as intellectual independence. Very early in Flavius's education the value of money was stressed: "I would advise you," his father wrote, "to pay some attention to business. I am afraid you are going to make a sort of a softly feminine man. I should be sorry after spending so much of my hard earnings to educate you to find at the expiration of your studies that you were not capable of getting a living."[25] He wanted his son to internalize the values of money and hard work which, when combined with temperance and diligence, gave the yeoman farmer of William Cook's generation his sense of pride and position in society. His letters resounded on this theme: "You do not know the worth of money as you never had to make any exertion for it." "I hope for my sake you will be very particular in making change." "I would be temperate in all things. Let cold water or good milk be your favorite drink." "I should want to know what becomes of my money? I wish you to consider every dollar that I send you worth as much as though you had earned it chopping cord wood."[26]

In the fall of 1858, at age twenty, Flavius Cook went off to Yale College. En route, Flavius made a pilgrimage to New York City, to see the sights and get a taste of the excitement of the nation's center for progressive activity. He went several times to hear Henry Ward Beecher, a champion of social reform, deliver his sermons in Plymouth Congregational Church, and also visited the great publisher, Horace Greeley. Immersing himself in the latest scientific and progressive fashions, he had his head "read" by a leading phrenologist (phrenology was associated with progressive science and politics in the mid–nineteenth century.)[27]

At Yale, young Cook busied himself with a wide variety of activities, including a student journal, which he founded. He began to have increased doubts about religion, which alarmed his parents, especially so as these doubts affected his mental health. His father wrote reassuringly that "the reading of H. W. Beecher's sermons would be food for you as they are for me. Let us obey our better judgments and do right in all things. We all lack faith, we all commit sin constantly." Yet Cook continued to have doubts and disregarded his father's advice, "Don't brood over the past and get gloomy."[28]

Flavius's father was also apprehensive about his son's becoming too deeply involved with a young woman, "Miss H," who in the father's eyes was nothing but trouble. "Strive to keep clear of trouble with your female acquanitance."[29] William Cook himself, his own wife lamented, cared little enough for female acquanitances: "Your pa . . . does just as everybody wants him to do, except me." "Pa very often says he had rather give [something special] away then to have me have it. . . ."[30] He was concerned lest women take what they should not have, and he also viewed them as threats to manhood itself: "All I can make out of it is that you have laid your head in some Delilah's lap and have been shorn of your strength."[31]

Although Flavius's mother had few of her own needs met, she was still concerned about whether her son was warm and comfortable. "I think you deserve a good scolding . . . a child of mine, all the one I have in the world . . . sleeps . . . without a pillow to lay his head on." "I want you to buy a pillow and send me word in particular that you have got one."[32] "Flave, have you put on your shirts with Marsailles bosoms and long wristbands? If not you must, and wear them through cold weather." In a curt note of motherliness, Ma wrote, "Get on flannel."[33]

Eventually, notwithstanding his father's reassurances and his mother's loving concern for his welfare, Flavius had a mental breakdown and had to leave college. In 1861, he was sent to the well-known McLean Asylum in Sommerville, Massachusetts, and placed under the care of John Tyler. A well-known director of sanitariums, Tyler believed that the major causes of insanity were increased commercial tension nationally as well as increased religious doubts. Environmental factors,then, explained breakdowns, and a proper environment free of tension and negative influences would cure the patient. Hence, patients at McLean were placed in a controlled environment.[34] For Flavius Cook, the treatment apparently worked: two years later he was out and enrolled at Harvard College. After graduating and changing his name to Joseph Cook, he went into the ministry, his religious doubts seemingly conquered. He attended Andover Theological Seminary and, after completing his studies with some distinction became minister in

Andover for a year before being called Lynn in 1870 to be acting minister of the First Congregational Church.

Lynn's First Congregational Church symbolized New England's solid middle class. Most of its members were respectably well off, being professionals, established merchants, and other townsfolk, with the city's manufacturers largely Quakers, Baptists or Episcopalians. They were aware of Lynn's phenomenal growth and prosperity—and also of the rising number of non-affiliated workers—and shared the values William Cook had tried to instill in his son.

Thanks to his father's efforts, Joseph Cook had no illusions about the life of the yeoman farmer: he knew that farm life consisted mostly of hard times and tight money, back-breaking work with little financial reward. He reshaped the paternal rural values of hard work, frugality, temperance, and diligence into a new intellectual framework as well as a vision of a new social structure that could reassure Lynn's confused and troubled middle class. This intellectual model incorporated traditional values into a new social order, one based not upon the isolated individual, but modeled on an army—a moral army, with the church as its head and the moral reformers as its generals.

THE INTELLECTUAL FRAMEWORK

The Civil War and the new industrial society with its opposing classes combined to overwhelm the world of the early-nineteenth-century social reformer, in which Joseph Cook had been deeply immersed. The old order had an ideal of the individual who, guided by an inner moral sense, could (in the words of his father) "take the lead," "work in [his] own harness, pattern after no man," and do "good to the world's teeming masses,"[35] by individual moral action. It had been destroyed first by the opposing armies of North and South and then by those of labor and capital. In neither the Civil War nor the industrial North was there room for the transcendental individual. New collective armies now decided moral issues and the individual had to find a new place in a new collective community. "I am no individualist," Joseph Cook stated in 1879: although "the old transcendentalists gave countenance to individualism like Mr. Emerson's" individualism had degenerated to "evolution and materialism." "The rationalistic transcendentalists have been of late thrown into panic," he continued, and although they "made bold marches in Boston 30 years ago", they have been "scattered and serried." Indeed, the movement that had given so much direction to middle-class America in the early nineteenth century was by his own assessment "substantially defeated."[36] Joseph Cook was concerned about this defeat, especially after it became clear that the world which had given rise to transcendentalism and its individualistic moral order no longer existed. Materialism and social evolution, as articulated by Herbert Spencer, became important altenative ideologies to transcendentalism during the rise of the new industrial society.[37]

The problem for Cook and his generation of middle-class Americans was to create a new model of social relations. The one adopted by Cook was based upon an army, the very vehicle that had destroyed the old worldview; for, in Cook's mind, society was increasingly resembling an army, armies of highly regimented workers and of industry. In that new regimentation, Cook found his vehicle for a new order of community: "Business is a regiment. For industrial reasons, men must keep step with each other in it. Let the majority of the Board of Trade of any city set right business fashions, and the inferior men who care only for money are usually brought sooner or later to respect the step of the regiment."[38] And at a later time Cook reiterated:

> The Church can set fashions for the upper ranks among leaders of business that is for the best men in it. In most of the great lines of industry business is a regiment. Men must keep step with each other: and if the Church can set the fashion for the upper twenty in every hundred businessmen, these upper twenty will set the step for the regiment.[39]

Although he was here talking about how to reform business and make it more moral, it is clear from his metaphor of the regiment that he perceived the new order of society as a means of recreating a moral order.

In practical terms Cook was very conscious, like the middle class generally, that industrialization created wealth and prosperity for Lynn and in turn for the middle class. "This city has greatly prospered in the last twenty years."[40] he wrote. "When the soldiers marched, Lynn clothed their feet; and the steel clad hoof of war smiting on the Lynn lap-stone struck forth here abundant sparks of prosperity."[42] As the son of an established but constantly struggling farmer, Cook appreciated the value of Lynn's prosperity. He realized that the new industrial city provided opportunity and progress unknown in the countryside. His father's constant reminders of debts and hard times, as well as his speculations about the benefits modern industry and the railroads would have on rural Ticonderoga, remained in Joseph's mind. "I am lost in stalk and debts," his father once confessed: "I must get out of this hard work if I have to sell my farm."[42] "I suppose we may say that they are to work on the railroads."[43] Yet, like Lynn's middle class, Joseph Cook was also concerned about the negative consequences of industrialization:

> ... The large factories have introduced an operative class and an employing class . . . Congregated labor and a large floating population are historically known as having always heretofore given rise in large towns to grave moral and industrial perils and abuses: and the new system of the shoe trade necessitates congregated labor; and the annual fluctuations of the activity of the trade give rise in large towns to a large floating population.[44]

Joseph Cook realized that the new industrial organization brought not only new wealth, but also new dangers. These dangers destroyed the old consciousness and community of independent artisans. "As a rule the old shoemakers were largely independent in the management of their business and each family attending to its own for itself. But the large factories have introduced an operative class and an employing class." This new world with opposing classes subverted the old individualistic ideal, shared by the independent artisans, which had inspired the transcendental worldview. It also created a "hereditary ignorant and unemployed class," with "slums [left] to fester and crowded tenement-houses packed with men and women as sardine boxes are packed with fish." The system spawned large urban areas where children "look out from their cradles into brothels, they hear the worst of men and women curs[ing] . . . each other. From their cradles your children grow worse."[45] Indeed, in these rising industrial cities "the system of modern manufacturers in large populations tends to produce a superior class and an inferior." The new system of factory organization then created a situation where "the accumulations of wealth fall chiefly to employers and not to operatives. The distance between the two classes is a result of deep causes arising from the two great laws of the manufacturing system." These laws—which Cook saw as the development of division of labor and the increase in size of the manufacturing establishments— "produce here . . . an employing class annd an operative class and perpetually tend to make the distance between rich and poor in manufacturing populations wider and wider."[46]

Such conflict not only broke up the old individualist community, Cook perceived, it posed a problem for the modern society: the organization of these growing opposing classes into a new comprehensive community. This problem was rooted in the economic structure: "I suppose that the deepest question yet remaining unsolved in this nation is that concerning the relations between capital and labor." And Cook, like most reformers and labor leaders, believed that "slavery itself was but one form of that question [the relations between capital and labor]." Indeed, he recognized that the relationship between capital and labor also involved "discontent of the working class!" "We hear the retreating footsteps of the discussions concerning slavery, and at the same time the advancing footsteps . . . of discussions concerning the working classes in crowded populations."[47]

SOCIETY AS REGIMENT

Having thoroughly frightened himself and his congregation by recounting the negative consequences of industrialization, Cook then juxtaposed them with the benefits of the new system in terms of its wealth and prosperity, while he proceeded to grope for a solution to the problems of labor–capital conflict and continual community discord. Cook did not offer Lynn, its workers, or its middle class, a new system of ordered production or a new method for the distribution of wealth. Instead, he accepted the process of private accumulation and capitalism. As he stated later in the decade, "Socialism, by destroying the right of personal ownership in the means of production and by fostering dependence on state help, undermines the spirit of self-help and so is a fatal enemy of the cause of the poor." "I am against socialistic arrangements,"[48] he categorically stated.

Cook also drew upon the old producer ideology and the labor theory of value for justification of the existing order: the "legitimacy of private property rests on the right inherent in every workman either to consume or to save the product of his labor. Producers have a right to what they have themselves produced." But in this scheme, Cook distinguished between the actions of the factory operative and the essence of the productive process. Indeed, he argued that the worker (unlike the manufacturer) did not have a right to the finished product because he/she "only gives form to costly materials which capital brought together."[49] Astonishingly, under Cook's model, giving form to raw materials did not constitute the creation of a product.

Since Cook was unwilling to endorse a new form for the organization of production, in response to what was perceived to be the dangers posed by the new industrialization, he was forced to search for an alternative prescription for society's ills. It led him back to the ideas of his old therapist, John Typer at the McLean Asylum, about the causes and cure of insanity. Tyler had conceptualized the problem of insanity as a product of environmental influences on the individual. A negative or tense environment created a condition of psychic imbalance. The cure for an individual's insanity required the elimination of the negative environment. Adopting the environmentalist model, Cook told his middle-class audiences that the problems of modern industrial society lay not in private control of the means of production, but in the factory and community environments, which were fashioning an immoral working class. What was required, then, was a new moral order. The problem was not that society was divided into classes, Cook proclaimed, but that the working class, having been exposed to negative environmental influences, was out of control and suffering from an increasingly immoral character.[50] A floating population of factory operatives, without the strong influences of a family environment or the individual discipline of the independent artisan, was getting out of control.

Given this diagnosis, Cook then reexamined the evils of the factory system and identified the numerous corrupting influences of the work environment: the "mingling of the sexes in the workrooms and carelessness as to the moral character of overseers" in workrooms where "men and women, boys and girls, gathered in large part at random out of a floating population are sandwiched together like herring in a box, uninterrupted by the noise of machinery, it is not infrequently foul talk, profanity, and tobacco smoke from morning to night." It was the factory, then, upon which Cook focused as the source of corruption, for this was, as he perceived it, a "foul system." Thus, he could admit the benefits of the system, in the wealth that it created, and yet attack it—not for creating divisions between the rich and poor, but for corrupting the workers. Its victims suffered a moral injury, not an economic inequity. Emphasizing its corrupting influence on the poor, Cook then argued for reforms to restore the moral purity of the corrupted class. Thus the focus shifted: the evils of the factory system derived not from class divisions and poverty, but from "undermining the good order in the working class and also undermining regularity of industry and diminishing the worth of the hours of labor."[51]

Cook's remedy drew on the old family hierarchy. It was a system of order that he imagined could be generalized in new forms:

It is impossible to speak too strongly of the worth of family life as a moral police in society. [The individual] comes home at night to a circle that know[s] him well and watch[es] his daily course, [he] has a kind of daily appearance to make before a moral tribunal. The bliss of the home affections is a shield from vice, not only because it is bliss, but because it makes any conduct that needs concealment from the moral tribunal of the most intimate circle as painful as the bliss of ingenuousness and trust is great.[52]

Although ideally the family could act as a moral police force and be part of a reordered new moral community, Cook admitted that in reality the family was becoming less meaningful because of an emerging "floating population" without ties to the community. Cook's new moral community had to be built upon a larger institution than the family. For this reason, he looked to the church, the schools, and new authoritarian structure in the factories themselves to fulfill this organizational vacuum.

Thus, the new community that Cook offered his audience did not deny the existence of class divisions but proposed a moral order, policed by the chuch and school, that transcended class lines and culminated in moral unity. In his mind, church and school transcended class divisions: "The church, which holds both rich and poor, . . . [is] a means of allaying prejudice and securing mutual understanding, justice, and good-will, [so] as to give it much the same relations to the different classes in society at large, as the Industrial Board of Arbitration or Conference has in particular cases of conflict."[53]

Cook's conception of unity contemplated a hierarchical moral structure that subordinated workers to employers. The Bible would serve as the source of the incipient moral order: "the chasm between capital and labor . . . can be bridged only by the Bible laid on the buttresses of the Sunday and the Common Schools." The fundamental organizing principle of Cook's new order was a "moral division of labor" in which the workers cooperated by developing traits of deference, obedience, and temperance, while the manufacturers provided leadership in the form of discipline, supervision, and control. Thus, he noted, for workers "the great principle of co-operation which is the hope of the cause of labor depends peculiarly for its success upon a high degree of self-control, integrity, and mutual confidence in moral character. . . . This self-control and moral confidence has been proved . . . to be the cement without which the stones in the temple of Co-operation most assuredly cannot be laid." Yet ironically he suggested that workers could achieve these virtues of self-control and integrity only if properly supervised and controlled by manufacturers, who were depicted as the moral elite. For this reason, Cook called upon employers to adopt more stringent means of social control over the work place: "Appoint men of irreproachable character as overseers and separate the sexes in the workrooms."[54] In effect, even his conception of cooperation seemed to be inspired by the authoritarian discipline characteristic of an army regiment. Such discipline seemed essential. The emerging industrial order, with large numbers of workers grouped together in a class, constituted a threatening reality. Although the middle class recognized that the social organization of the factory demanded an army of workers, it also feared that the army might turn against the society.

The reforms advocated by Cook promised not only to create a new authoritarian community, to replace the individualistic model of the transcendentalist, but also to generate more wealth for this community. For his new disciplined workers would be more ordered and, theoretically, more productive. In practical terms Cook's ideals meant increased church attendance, more temperance reform, separation of the sexes in the factories, and greater control over primary-school education and boardinghouses; they appealed to middle-class morality. So, too, did his quintessentially Victorian image of womanhood, which the new industrial order seemed to threaten:

> It is found by experience that it is in the workroom that a young woman coming here and not resisting . . . the morally unhealthful influences, loses that natural shyness and modesty which are her charm, and gradually acquires a repulsive boldness. There are spiritual and physical signs of every vice. The loss of spiritual shyness and nobleness can be seen, as well as the loss of natural freshness of complexion and of a lusterful flash of the eye.[55]

The traditional definition of womanhood did not extend to female labor, but rather emphasized woman as homemaker and protected innocent. Cook, however, accepted the reality of working women and attempted to superimpose the image of the Victorian woman, placing it in this new factory context. Women could work, but only under strict controls. Lynn's working women could maintain their womanhood by being deferential and being supervised by moral overseers. This attempt to reassert the conventional image was not simply an accommodation to the reality of female labor; on the contrary, it directly challenged the working-class women's claim of their importance to society and, during the 1860 strike, of their refusal to "be slaves."[56]

The new moral community envisioned by Cook accorded the middle class a special role, serving as the agent of reform. This class would act as a "powerful public sentiment, or moral conscience which would influence the better class of men." Increasingly threatened by the development of a social system that excluded it, the middle class, "the masses of members of churches," could become a major force in Cook's plan to control society and safeguard the reform movement. "[There is a] vast amount of unexpressed sympathy [for labor reform and temperance by the middle class], now largely wasted, . . . which a right use of the Sabbath by working men might do much, directly and indirectly, to turn into channels of the very highest value to those [interests]."[57] Within this new society, modeled on a military structure, the business leaders were to be the captains, but the middle class, the collective moral conscience, would be the general overseeing the institutions of social control, particularly the church and schools.[58]

Although the society that Cook described was a hierarchial, highly regimented, authoritarian system, it also retained a deep commitment to the concept of individualism. Cook and many other nineteenth-century reformers were concerned with the traditional, increasingly irrelevant, concept of individualism. The new society was organized around factory production and regimentation and had to demand discipline, having less and less room for the individualist. Ideologically, however, it was a society founded upon the concept of individualism.

But a new conception of individualism replaced the one on the wane. It was based not upon independence but upon mobility. It presupposed a hierarchical collective, an army that allowed superior individuals to move up through the ranks. Indeed, loyalty to the system became the new means of manifesting individualism. The individual who demonstrated loyalty, obedience, and productivity was recognized by occupational and societal promotion. Thus individualism was transformed into the ideology of upward mobility, which could also serve as a social control mechanism by discouraging more radical solutions premised upon working-class actions in the interest of social justice.

Later in the 1870s Joseph Cook made this position explicit, arguing that socialism fails "by destroying the right of personal ownership in the means of production and by fostering dependence on state-help, [which] undermines the spirit of self-help and so is a fatal enemy of the cause of the poor." God, he asserted, created differences among people so that they could use their own abilities to move themselves upward: "Men are sent into the world with different endowments," and "so long as private property is allowed to exist there will be great inequalities in the distribution of wealth." But the success of an individual "depends upon self-help." And that success is a positive force in society. "Society needs cooperation and industrial partnership and the self-inspired mobility of labor."[59]

In May, 1872, Joseph Cook finished his lecture series in Lynn and journeyed to Germany to further his studies. A major center of philosophical thought, Germany had a strong appeal for Americans looking for theoretical guides in the bewildering world of the late nineteenth century. It offered exposure to both progressive ideas and experimental social welfare policies. Cook studied at Halle, Leipzig, Berlin, and Heidelberg, where he was influenced by the German evangelical movement. After a tour through Europe, Cook returned to the United States and began a series of weekly lectures in Boston's Tremont Temple. These lectures not only earned him a considerable income between 1875 and 1895, but also attracted the largest audiences in Boston's history.

Although orthodox in their theology and in their attacks against biblical critics, evolutionists, and freethinkers, Cook's lectures also reiterated the themes that Cook had begun to articulate in Lynn. They helped to popularize the concepts that society was increasingly divided between rich and poor and that the role of the church was to champion the cause of the poor. They also continued to emphasize the notion that salvation of the poor could only be achieved by the rejection of socialism and adherence to a strict moral code. Cook vividly described the importance of improving the conditions of the poor through the creation of a strictly controlled moral order, in which labor and capital formed a partnership under the supervision of the church, which served as moral and social arbitrator.

Most of the lectures, which were published either as pamphlets or books, reflect Cook's intention of having middle-class Americans lead a conservative reform movement, which would restructure society under church direction. Indeed, he even called for the creation of a "theocracy" to control the radical potential of popular democracy. Although not insisting on the abandonment of all democratic institutions, Cook was convinced that saving society meant strict social control in terms of moral rather than physical coercion: "If America leaves slums to fester, and crowds tenement houses with men and women as sardine-boxes are packed with fish, and allows the just demands of labor to go unanswered . . . then even military might won't help. . . . Public schools and churches and not gattling guns are to be the delivery of America from socialistic abuse of Universal Sufferage."[60]

Commenting on Cook's advocacy of moral reform as the mechanism for social transformation, one observer has claimed that Cook "probably did more than any other individual or group in bringing the social implications of Christianity to the attention of Americans."[61] Certainly Cook's legacy included a unique diagnosis of and prescription for working-class conditions, an "environmental" or "ecological" method of analysis, and the dissemination of a social gospel, all of which endorsed reform as an alternative to radical change. His popularization of these themes fueled the growing fear in the middle class that a rising, environmentally inferior lower class would pass on that inferiority; this fear in turn fueled the social gospel movement and, later, progressivism. Cook's imagery and concerns reappeared in the work of such diverse figures as Jacob Riis, with his concern for the dangerous nature of an oppressed "other half," and George Bellamy, with his socialist utopia built around Army metaphor. Although Cook himself faded from the national scene in the late 1890s, his concern for reform, social control, and theological conservatism remained a major part of the American middle-class world.[62]

Cook's vision of society was an appealing one for members of the First Congregational Church and for Lynn's middle class generally. Hundreds crowded into the newly built Music Hall* to hear him, and although some objected vehemently to what he said (even to the point of violence, including a major scuffle and more than one arrest), the largely middle-class audience applauded and rallied around the concept of moral reform. As reported at the time, Cook's lectures not only "aroused [the] community as no other occurrence [had in] a long time," they also struck a responsive chord in the middle-class community. The congregation's approval was reflected in the praise Cook received when his lectures were completed, and the expressions "of high regard which the congregation entertained [for him.]"[63]

The middle class were not the only members of the Lynn community concerned about the factory system and interested in Joseph Cook's lectures on factory reform. Both the older artisans, who had been displaced by the factories, and the unskilled women and immigrants whose lives had been shaped by the factory system, felt compelled to respond to the new system of production.

The old cordwainers' world was shattered by the new factory system. No longer could a journeyman expect to move into a position as an independent artisan. The tremendous productive capacity of the new form of organization and the new machines eliminated the potential for the artisan to control his own shop. The artisan in the post–Civil War period was forced either to work for one of the large manufacturers or to abandon his trade entirely. Although some of the older shoe workers tried to compete with the large manufacturers, and

---

*The Music Hall was built in 1870 in Central Lynn, and when, in that year, the First Congregational Church burned down, the Music Hall was used for church purposes as it was for other major events in the city.

others were able to gain access to enough capital to become manufacturers themselves, most were forced to accept their new role as employees. The adjustment to that new role caused the skilled artisans considerable dislocation. Some clung to the old ideas of independence and the producers' ideology, which stressed that artisans and manufacturers were the producers of the wealth of society and as such shared a community of interest against the merchants and speculators. Others who found in their new relationship with the manufacturers conflict and antagonism, salvaged from the producers' ideology the concept of the labor theory of value, and argued that workers had to organize collectively to demand from manufacturers a greater share of the value produced.

Not all those who found themselves in the new factory buildings came from artisan traditions. Many of the unskilled, particularly women and immigrants, were not deeply rooted in the artisan tradition or the producer ideology. They relied upon their position in the factories as the sole source of their livelihood. When the manufacturers reduced wages and increased the work expected from the employees, these workers joined the union movement, particularly the Knights of St. Crispin, and allied themselves with those skilled workers who rejected the idea that a community of interest existed between the manufaturers and the workers.

Lynn working-class activists organized a local chapter of the Knights and Daughters of St. Crispin, a national organization of shoe workers. Cultivating workers' hostility toward manufacturers, and developing the insights first experienced in the strike of 1860, these activists insisted that tension would always exist between workers and manufacturers because the factory system enslaved workers while it enriched the owners. Seeking out the unskilled laborers who lodged in the cramped quarters bordering the central city manufacturing district and who sought respite from their labors in the bars, taverns, and cafes of the central city, the Crispins disseminated their proposals for factory reform through informal gatherings and through the publication of a labor paper, *The Little Giant*.

Initially, the Crispins envisioned Cook as an ally in the struggle for factory reform. "We commend him for his frank outspoken style and for the interest which he appeared to take in the labor question and the general welfare of the masses," stated the editors of *The Little Giant*. As Cook began to emphasize the moral inferiority of the working class in general and of working women in particular, the labor paper abandoned its initial support for Cook and urged workers to rely upon themselves rather than moral reformers for an improvement in their condition. "The moral status of the employees in the shop in question is reputed to be especially good," it declared, "and it seems incredible that a man professing the Gospel should wantonly assail the characters of innocent females who earn their daily toil." And it continued, "He owes an apology to the ladies in the shop and justice demands that he should make it." While Cook saw the women in the shop as degraded and immoral, needing an authoritarian hand to keep them deferent and modest, activists in the labor movement saw them as "respectable, hard working women." Ultimately, these labor activists rejected not only Cook's analysis of the moral condition of the workers but also his vision of a morally ordered hierarchical society. Instead, they described a class-riddled society in which the labor force would unite in opposition to capital: "We would caution the working men against the effects of heated discussions on this subject, for discussions and differences in their ranks will lead to a disastrous result. Remember the old motto: 'United we stand, Divided we fall.' "[64]

Although the Crispins spoke for a large and growing number of workers in the city, not all of the cordwainers accepted their analysis. Many, particularly those with long ties to the older institutions of the community (particularly the Protestant churches) did not follow the Crispins' advice. These older artisans saw in Cook's call for a moral community a means of ascribing status to themselves independent of their role in the production process. Cook's moral reform movement enabled them to resurrect the older idea of a community of interest between the workers and the manufacturers rather than to accept the vision of a class-divided society. One worker noted that he felt Cook "was talking for the best good of the laboring class, and they pretty generally so understood it." He continued that he "did not believe in the Crispin organization [since] he was opposed to a monopoly of muscle, just as much as to a monopoly of money." Maintaining an image of a harmony of interests among competitors, this commentator rejected the idea that collective organization by workers would aid them and claimed that in fact it would "injure the working class more than any one else." In the same vein, he suggested that the strike of 1860 had injured the workers more than the manufacturers.[65] Some two hundred workers signed a petition supporting Cook's lectures and call for moral reform. These workers identified with neither the organization of the new working class nor with the manufacturers. They endorsed Cook's attacks on the immorality of the unskilled workers, as well as his attacks on the greediness of the manufacturers. As an articulation of their suspicion and hostility toward both groups, Cook's depiction of the evils of both groups afforded these nonaligned artisans the comfort of clinging to the moral superiority of their economically outmoded form of manufacture.

Cook's popularity among the older artisans was mitigated by his unpopularity among the unskilled immigrants, who found themselves described as immoral. In response to his comments on the immorality of employees in one of the city's factories, a group of employees wrote a letter in self-defense to the local paper. They noted that there was "nothing to condemn them but that they [were] compelled to labor for their own maintenance." Suspecting that Cook's comments were implicitly directed against the Irish Catholics, the pastor of St. Mary's Church, the Reverend Patrick Strain, added his name to those who felt Cook had unjustly attacked people whose only crime was to work as unskilled laborers. The pastor supported Cook's call for a reform of the factory system, but qualified that support by asking for a committee of *all* churches to deal with the issue of moral reform. Moreover, Father Strain took exception to Cook's attacks on the moral character of Lynn's workers. "I say that this charge is a detraction and a calumny on the working girls and men of this city."[66]

Although Cook's cricitism of the factory system was never directed against capital accumulation or the exploitation of labor, Lynn's entrepreneurs felt that his perceptions of the increasing divisions between capital and labor and his characterization of the factory system itself demanded a response. Not only did the manufacturers Bubier and Frazier attack Cook's characterization of the factory system as leading to immorality, but the manufacturers organized a competing lecture on the factory system, entitled "The Labor Interests of Lynn." The President of the Board of Trade, George Keene, who was also a leading manufacturer, used this series as a forum for the presentation of an alternative view of the factory system. Keene argued that the new mode of production provided for more social benefits than burdens. "We have been called upon to introduce an entire change in our mode of manufacturing," and this change has added prosperity and wealth to the city. He cited upward mobility as one of the outstanding goods created by the new factory system: "Our prosperous manufacturers are men from the common walks of life, who after toiling and struggling with the vicissitudes of business, are themselves the controlling power, and personally interested in our [the city's] success." These humble origins explained the existence of the community of interest between producers and workers: "There is . . . a kindly sympathy between the manufacturer and his workmen. . . . It is in the nature of business to bring manufacturer and workmen into harmony, because their interests are identical." The worldview of the manufacturers, although not opposed to that of Cook, stressed the commonality of experience between the rich and the poor, rather than the divisions between the two classes: "There is in Lynn no aristocracy of wealth or family. The leading men of Lynn show prominently to the world that with us the poor of to-day will be the rich of tomorrow. This harmony of interests in Lynn is manifested by the meetings and friendly consultations of both parties."[67]

Despite the variety of responses to Cook's lectures, the lectures were clearly a success. Cook managed to fill the seats of the Music Hall and revitalize the First Congregational Church. The issues first addressed by Cook in Lynn in 1871 did not disappear with Cook's departure for Europe in the spring of the year. Cook later returned to an America that increasingly resembled the Lynn that he had left. That America was ready to hear the message of social and moral reform first preached by Cook in Lynn. Cook's lectures in Boston proved even more successful than those in Lynn. Cook's conservative ideas about the ordering of society, coupled with his call for moral reform, won widespread support. Ultimately those who took up the call for reform and social control went further and gained more national prominence than Cook, but the seeds for that movement were sown in the Music Hall of a small industrial city, which itself was in the vanguard of industrializing America.

Because of his concern for the negative impact of the environment on the working class and because he came to believe that environmental factors affect intelligence and even heredity, Cook's lectures included a detailed description of the industrial environment. He explored the work place, the structure of the city, the change in the nature of the work force, the statistical makeup of the work force, and the nature of the family. Like any good environmentalist, Cook was an observer and detailed chronicler of the industrial environment. We may not agree with his conclusions, and some of his data may have been distorted. Yet the lectures are an important and rich source of information not only about Cook, the middle class, and social reform, but also about the conditions of labor and the organization of the shoe and textile industries. They also describe the industrial revolution in the shoe industry and the impact of that revolution on the social structure of a community.

When the lectures are read a distinction should be maintained between Joseph Cook, the observer and chronicler of an industrial city, and Joseph Cook, the product of nineteenth-century Protestant America with all the biases and prejudices of that society. His description of the floating population, for example, although a correct description of the increased mobility, youth, and lack of ties of the growing operative class, also includes within it a biased assumption that these individuals were qualitatively different from past artisans in ways other than those of youth and mobility. Indeed, there is an implication that they are different partly because they are more likely to be foreign born, Catholic, Irish, and inherently inferior. Cook is subtle enough not to state this explicitly, yet the context of his lectures and the nature of the audience he was addressing enabled him to convey this intent without the need for an explicit statement. The rector of the predominantly Catholic St. Mary's Church quickly came to the defense of the "poor, honest, industrious, and defenseless girls,"[68] indicating that he too saw the attack on the immorality of the workers as a not-too-veiled attack against Irish Catholics. This bias is made even clearer when Cook distinguishes between American workers and Catholic workers.

Another example of Cook's bias is his use of sexual suggestions. When Cook alludes to the "infamous diseases," he means venereal disease. He then uses venereal disease to imply sexual intercourse in order to excite the prurient interests of his audience. He alludes to the fact that these "infamous diseases" can spread to the middle classes by way of sexual liaisons between middle-class husbands and prostitutes or promiscuous operatives. He never formally states this to be the case but makes his point through implication and through parallels with tuberculosis. "When the operative's fever broke out into the middle classes in old England under the old factory system . . . the abuses in the mills that had been overlooked while only the operatives suffered, were remedied almost exclusively from fear of contagion in other classes."[69] Cook was not referring to tuberculosis but to venereal disease in his lectures. The use of inference and the fear of venereal disease was a classic Victorian method of both interesting the audience and producing concern over the issue under discussion. Its use here by Cook probably tells us more about Victorian attitudes towards sex, prostitution, and social codes than it does about the actual physical condition of the operative class, although venereal disease was a fairly widespread problem during that time (see note on page 75).

The Music Hall Lectures are presented in sequential form as they were originally delivered. Some of the Reverend Mr. Cook's words have been eliminated, especially where redundant. Those lectures for which verbatim records are not available are presented as newspaper transcriptions (Lectures 4, 6, 7, 8, 9); the others are, as far as possible, reprinted in their entirety. Spelling has been modernized and punctuation corrected where it was thought that the original would obscure rather than clarify the meaning.

In response to the Reverend Mr. Cook, the manufacturers of Lynn established an alternate lecture to which Cook himself replied. This lecture and other contemporary responses are presented in the last chapter. The reader should pay particlar attention to these responses in order to appreciate the full impact of Cook's lectures.

Specific lectures and responses have been provided with explanatory introductions, where needed. Readers who desire more information about the topics considered in either the introductions or lectures should refer to the bibliography at the end of the book. Portions of the lectures may be confusing to the modern reader or may for other reasons deserve specific comment; such comments and explanations appear as footnotes at the bottom of the pertinent page of text. Cook's original footnotes have been retained, bracketed, and incorporated into the text of the lectures.

2

The Lectures of the Reverend Joseph Cook

INTRODUCTION TO LECTURE 1

The Reverend Joseph Cook, having announced his topic to be "Moral Perils of the Present Factory System of Lynn," entered the Music Hall to find a full house with over one hundred persons standing and others turned away at the door. Cook began his lecture series in January, when little else was going on in the city for entertainment, but to keep his audience he had to be both exciting and provocative. His first lecture met both requirements.

Cook began with a short history of the process of industrialization in Lynn. He made nostalgic reference to the old days of the craftsmen ("Old Lynn") and proceeded to document, with extensive statistics, the industrial change not only in Lynn but in the nation itself. Cook's extensive use of statistics, which were so important to social investigators of the late nineteenth century, supplied the "scientific" base for his arguments. He then attacked the new manufacturing system for breeding immorality while praising it for producing wealth and power unknown to "Old Lynn." Cook did not suggest an alternative industrial system, and all reforms he proposed were well within the realm of the existing system. Yet his attack on the immorality of mixing male and female operatives and of allowing improper language in the factories, and his forays against the moral character of some of the city's overseers, were so dramatic and forceful as to appear "bold and vigorous." And they produced a storm of protest within the city: Cook's opposition to the evils of the existing system aroused the anger of the manufacturers. At the same time his call for more social control to prevent the rise of "the discontent of the working class" also won him considerable sympathy from those who did not reject the private industrial system, but who feared the changes which that system brought with it.

1. THE MORAL PERILS OF THE PRESENT FACTORY SYSTEM OF LYNN

Extraordinary Recent Growth of Lynn

This city has been greatly prospered [sic] in the last twenty years. In 1850 your population was thirteen thousand. Now it is twenty-nine thousand. In 1850 the valuation of your property was four million dollars. Now it is twenty million dollars. For the sixty years from 1795 to 1855, the increase of the value of the productions of your great branch of industry was, every ten years, one hundred per cent. For the ten years from 1855 to 1865, the increase of that value was three hundred per cent. [Census of Massachusetts, 1865.] When the soldiers marched, Lynn clothed their feet; and the steel-clad hoof of war, smiting on the Lynn lap-stone, struck forth here abundant sparks of prosperity.

I blame no man for being proud of the recent secular advances of Lynn. The time has been when there was altogether too little local pride here. One of the speakers at the dedication of your city hall, an ex-mayor, said that the local remark used to be that all Lynn was mortgaged to a neighboring city. That day has passed. There is a New Lynn. It is visible enough in the midst of Old Lynn. The city hall costing three hundred and fifty thousand dollars, new schoolbuildings, new churches, new business blocks, new factories, fifty-five railway trains a day, have made a New Lynn. And Old Lynn, with its poorer achitecture, lies in the arms of New Lynn, as the old moon, which I saw in the west as I came to this meeting, lies in the arms of the crescent new moon: a crescent, indeed, as yet, but sure to become a sphere.

I care for Lynn. I recognize its prosperity and its general good order. But, in spite of this, for what I say tonight I expect to be cut into more pieces than you ever cut leather into in your factories.

*The Right Organization of the Largest Trade of the United States,
of Hardly Less Than National Importance.*

Wholly aside, however, from the local importance of the extraordinarily delicate and complicated theme which I am to bring before you, there are other and far larger considerations which make its discussion, and its discussion at the present time, of high moment.

Five reasons exist why the right organization of the new factory system of the vast trade of this city, is of altogether more than local, and of hardly less than national importance. The circumstances need only to be named to exhibit their own commanding significance. My personal motives for entering upon the discussion of this evening will undoubtedly be variously construed. I profess that I have no other motives than those which are drawn from the five circumstances I am about to name. I am sure that I need no other and no greater.

1. There are more people engaged in the shoe trade than in any other single branch of manufactures in the United States, not excepting the coal, the iron, the woolen, or the cotton.

The unpoetic shoe trade happens to be the largest single branch of manufactures in the United States. "The manufacture of boots and shoes," says the preliminary report of the Eighth Census, "employs a larger number of operatives than any other single branch of American industry." [Preliminary Report on the Eighth Census of the United States, p. 68.] It is difficult to understand the importance of this fact except by a few statistical contrasts. Take the coal, the iron, the woolen, and the cotton trade. Every one recognizes these as vast and permanent public interests. They fill the land with the noise of hammers and spindles. Whatever affects powerfully the interests of either of these vast branches of industry is a matter of little less than national importance. The right organization of the industrial life of either of these trades would be a problem of commanding weight and interest. But the shoe trade employs a greater number of operatives than either of these other vast trades, taken alone. I find that in 1860 the entire list of woolen manufactures in the United States employed only 48,900 operatives. Of these, 28,780 were males and 20,120 females. The number of operatives employed in the cotton manufactures of the United States in 1860, I find, was only 118,920. Of these, 45,315 were males and 73,605 females. But, by the same census which gives these estimates, the number of hands employed in the United States in the manufacture of boots and shoes in 1860 was 127,427. Of these, 96,287 were males and 31,140 females. Even before the immense increase which the war brought to the shoe trade, the contrast of that branch of manufactures with the cotton, gives predominance to the former, by the difference between 118,920 operatives on the one hand and 127,427 on the other. [Ibid., Tables No. 22, No. 23, and No. 25, pp. 65–69, 180–185.]

In Massachusetts, taken alone, the shoe trade is vastly larger than any other; and this in spite of the fact that Lawrence and Lowell lead the cotton manufactures of the whole nation. This commonwealth in 1860 employed in the manufacture of cotton goods, 34,988 operatives. Of these, 12,635 were males and 22,353 were females. In the manufacture of boots and shoes it employed, in the same year, 69,398 operatives. Of these, 47,353 were males and 22,045 females. [Ibid., pp. 180, 185.]

This largest trade of the United States is rapidly increasing in size. In the journey of growth it moved its tents* with vast strides, not only during the war, but before. It is an exceedingly significant fact that, in 1860, 2,554 establishments engaged in this manufacture in the New England States employed a capital only $2,516 less than the whole Union employed in the manufacture in 1850. [Eighth Census, Preliminary Report, p. 68.] The entire value of the business of these establishments in 1860 was 82.8 per cent in excess of its value in 1850. New England, New York, Pennsylvania, and New Jersey together produced in 1860, 67.9 per cent more in value than in 1850. In this manufacture Massachusetts increased the value of its products, between 1850 and 1860, at the astonishing rate of 92.6 per cent. [Ibid., p. 68. Also Table 25.] I give these facts to exhibit the prosperity of the trade immediately before the war. But it is notorious that during the war, under the double impulse of the demands of the armies and the invention of new machinery for the manufacture, its rate of progress was yet more surprising. It has not shown any want of prosperity since the war. When the products of this trade in 1865 are put into contrast with those of 1870, the figures in Philadelphia are 605,329 compared with 2,111,024; and, in this city, 2,373,203 compared with 6,356,166.

Here, therefore, is a vast public interest; and whoever examines it is not discussing a trivial theme. It is exceedingly important, however, to notice not only that the theme is important, but that its discussion at the present, rather than at a later period, has an importance second only to that of the theme itself.

The Present a Period of Transition to a Wholly New Factory System.

2. On account of the recent invention of new machinery for its processes, this whole vast branch of manufactures throughout the United States is now in a condition of transition from the small shop system to the large factory system; it is adopting industrial arrangements which are likely to be a precedent for an extended and most important future; and the present, therefore, is the time to strike for the right crystalization of a factory system affecting the industrial and moral interests of a larger number of people than are reached by any other single branch of manufactures in the United States.

*Notice Cook's military metaphor.

Rapidity and Extent of the Changes Necessitated
by Recent Mechanical Inventions.

It is a matter of public notoriety that within the last ten years the methods of the shoe manufactures have been revolutionized by the invention of the McKay sewing machine. The invention of the spinning jenny and of the power loom did no more to revolutionize the cotton manufacture; the invention of the steam engine no more to change the methods of inland and maritime conveyance, than the application of the sewing machine to the shoe trade has done to revolutionize the processes of that branch of industry. The change has been as remarkable for rapidity as for extent. It was hastened by the great exigencies of our civil war. The celebrated machine which is likely to be remembered in history side by side with the spinning jenny and the power loom was invented and patented by Lyman R. Blake of South Abington, in this Commonwealth, as late as the year 1858. [Shoe and Leather Record, Boston, Sept. 26, 1870.] When the civil struggle began, it was seen that machinery must do the work of the multitudes of mechanics of the North, who had left their places and were fighting the battles of the war. The original patent was sold to Mr. Gordon McKay and Mr. J. G. Bates of Boston, for ten thousand dollars. It was somewhat improved by them. Not far from the second year of the war, it began to be applied to the shoe manufactures in establishments in this city. It is unnecessary to recite the rest of the history. Invention has followed invention. The supply of the wants of the new system of factories has tasked the skill of the best experts in machinery in New England. The McKay sewing machine, the skiving machine, the pegging machine, the sole-molding machine, the cable-wire machine, the self-feeding eyelet machine, are but a fraction of the recent inventions not only patented, but in use. Any list of machines correct for to-day is likely to be incorrect, because outgrown, to-morrow. Rapid as the supply of the new machinery has been, the demand for it has exceeded, and yet exceeds, the supply.

Three large results have followed this invention of new machinery. First, the small shop system has been abandoned and the large factory system has been adopted. Secondly, a great subdivision of labor has taken place. Thirdly, the trade is much more subject to lulls, or inactive seasons, than it was before the invention of the new machinery.

Occurring in the largest trade of the United States, these changes are events of a high order of public importance.

The transition from the old system to the new is complete and final. All Eastern Massachusetts is sprinkled thick with the small shoe shops, buildings twelve or twenty feet square, in each of which ten or fifteen men were usually employed on the heavier work of the trade, the females, in their own rooms at home, doing the lighter work. These buildings have been vacated, never to be filled again. For a hundred years they have been almost as characteristic of a large part of the towns of Eastern Massachusetts as the schoolhouses or the churches. The large factories, which are rising to fill their places, are destined to become larger and larger. There is no longer any artisan in this trade who makes a whole shoe. Subdivision of labor is sometimes carried so far that a single article passes through the hands of fifty workmen, each of whom is trained only to make a part. As a rule, the old shoemakers were largely independent in the management of their business, each family attending to its own for itself. But the large factories have introduced an operative class and an employing class. In the old system, work was commonly steady from year's end to year's end; or affected only by the larger fluctuations of general commerce. But now there are two periods in each year in the trade in any large city when hundreds of operatives are dropped from employment. So far apart at so many points are the old system and the new, that it is of little service to reason from the experience of the trade under the former system to the experience it is to expect under the new. It matters little if a man have passed a lifetime under the old system. He must judge the new system by the experiences developed under it, and not by the old.

The New System Likely To Become a Precedent.

It is of very great importance, while these changes are passing, to call attention in time to the high duty of setting right precedents in the new system. Let the first twenty years of the new order of things, or the first ten, be managed carelessly, and the needle will be threaded wrong for fifty years and will not be threaded wholly aright for a hundred. A responsibility of an extent and weight not easily overestimated, rests upon the manufacturing and operative classes who are now organizing a completely new factory system for the largest trade of the nation.

Lynn Leads the Trade.

3. This city leads this largest trade of the United States, which is now in a condition of transition to a new system; and the fashions which shall be set here for that new system have more than a local importance.

In 1860 Philadelphia led this trade. But Lynn has now led it for ten years. The largest business of any one town, in 1860, was that of Philadelphia, in which the production amounted to $5,329,887. Next came Lynn, in which the goods were valued at $4,867,399. Then followed Haverhill,* with a production of $4,130,500. Fourth, came New York, in which the products of the trade were valued at $3,869,068. [Eighth Census, Preliminary Report, p. 69.]

But Lynn has surpassed every other city in this branch of manufactures by the rapidity with which her factories have introduced the new machinery. The patent on the McKay machine secures to the proprietors the payment of a small royalty for every pair of shoes manufactured by the aid of this invention. It is of extreme interest, by figures that are already open to the inspection of the trade, that of all the shoes sewed upon the McKay sewing machines in the whole country, in 1870, twenty-eight per cent came from this city alone. In 1870, the amount paid in royalties to the proprietors of this machine was for the whole Union $400,011.08. Of this sum there was paid from this city $112,924.48, or more than a quarter of the whole.

Suppose that this city led the coal trade, or the iron. You would have a responsible position. Suppose it led the woolen or the cotton. You would have a position more responsible. But your present position is more responsible than even the latter. Suppose that this city led either the coal, the iron, the woolen, or the cotton trade, and that new inventions were to revolutionize the processes of industry in that trade and that you were called to adopt a new system. Your present position is more responsible still.

Distinction Between the Fluctuating and the Uninterrupted Industries.

4. In the article produced by the shoe trade there are, and in those produced by the coal, iron, woolen, and cotton trades there are not, annual fluctuations of fashion; hence the former trade is, and the latter are not, subject to annual fluctuations of activity; and, for this and other reasons, the shoe towns and the shoe factory system are not parallels of the cotton towns and the cotton factory system, and the new system cannot meet its exigencies by copying the methods of the old.

I beg leave to make a distinction between the fluctuating and the uninterrupted industries. More than one problem is explained for the student of the high theme of the moral and industrial economy of cities, by this distinction.

*Haverhill was another shoe-factory town in Massachusetts similar to but somewhat smaller than Lynn.

Certain trades produce articles in the very nature of which there are constant and wide changes of fashion. Evidently these articles cannot be accumulated in advance, for the fashions cannot be foreseen at any great distance. A stock of outgrown fashions on the market might ruin these trades. As soon as certain annual fashions are set for the articles, these industries have a period of extraordinary activity. When the demand is supplied, a period of comparative inactivity follows until the next set of fashions is determined. If fashions fluctuate annually, these trades fluctuate annually. If fashions fluctuate twice annually, these trades fluctuate twice annually. On the other hand, it is evident that if a trade produces an article in the very nature of which there does not exist this susceptibility to a change of fashion, it may work from year's end to year's end, and accumulate, if need be, a stock of its own products.

The latter is the condition of the coal, iron, woolen, and cotton trades. The former is the condition of the shoe trade.

All trades producing articles of clothing are subject in large towns to vast annual fluctuations of activity. In Boston, for example, the length of the working season for tailors and tailoresses is estimated at ten months; for shop work, at ten; for paper collar makers, at ten; for hosiery and rubber and elastic goods, at ten; for hatters, at eight; for corset makers and hoop-skirt makers, at seven and a half; and for straw workers, at seven. It seems a mystery that so many workmen worthy in every way, and sure to find difficulty or distress because unable to obtain occupation elsewhere, are dropped mercilessly from these employments by the thousands, at certain periods of the year. The explanation is simply that these employments produce articles subject to wide, annual, and unforeseen changes of fashion, and cannot accumulate stock in advance that is likely to be outgrown. We are often comfortably told that the wages given in such employments are of fabulous rates by the day or week. This is not often the case; but, even if it were, for how many weeks in the year does the working season hold?

There is another class of fluctuating industries in which the variations of activity arise from the changes of the seasons. Thus the length of the year is estimated for quarry workmen at ten months; for farm laborers, at eight; for masons, painters, and plasterers, at eight; for brickmakers, at seven.

Now it happens that the largest trade of the United States produces an article notoriously subject, especially in the varieties requiring the most delicate and skillful work, to wide changes of fashions; and those fashions themselves are largely affected by the changes of the seasons.

Both the great causes, therefore, which produce variations in the fluctuating as distinct from the uninterrupted industries, powerfully affect the largest trade of the United States.

Lynn works but about ten months a year. Lawrence and Lowell work twelve.*

This indicates the most fundamental distinction between the large cotton towns and the large shoe towns. Many give it as their judgment that the working season here does not exceed nine months.

You will mend these lulls, you say? Hundreds of years the artisans in other fluctuating industries which I have just named have tried to mend the lulls in large towns in their trades. They have not succeeded. To do so would be to counteract a natural law. Not one only but each of the great natural causes of fluctuation so affects the shoe trade in large towns, that I see no prospect of the lulls in it being soon removed; neither do any of the manufacturers with whom I have conversed. Rapidity of production being one of the causes of the lulls, it is found that as machinery becomes more perfect, the working season tends to become shorter. Machinery grows more perfect every day. It is introduced into large towns more promptly and abundantly than into small.

In a city establishment containing, for example, operatives enough to produce twenty sets, or twelve hundred pairs of shoes a day, the manager gives out stock enough in the morning to make only twelve or fifteen sets. As the brisk season of work arrives, stock enough is given out to make thirty or thirty-five sets a day, and more help engaged if it can be found. But, as the season of inactivity comes on, the stock is diminished again. Perhaps with a working capacity of twenty sets a day, only enough stock will be given out for twelve or ten sets. Of course, workmen drag on without half enough work for a while; and, finally, are unoccupied by the thousands.

Precisely here arise the chief industrial perils of the operative class in this branch of manufactures. Precisely here is the origin of large floating populations, with their attendant startling moral perils.

Perils of Congregated Labor in Large Towns.

5. Congregated labor and a large floating population are historically known as having always heretofore given rise in large towns to grave moral and industrial perils and abuses; and the new system of the shoe trade necessitates congregated labor; and the annual fluctuations of the activity of the trade give rise in large towns to a large floating population.

*Lawrence and Lowell, originally model textile towns, are described in Appendix A.

*English Factory Legislation an Illustration of These Perils.**

Sir Robert Peel told the English Parliament in 1816 that unless the tendency of congregated labor under the factory system in large towns to give rise to perils and abuses, could be corrected by decisive legislation, the great mechanical inventions, which were the glory of the age, would be a curse rather than a blessing to the country. [Hansard's Parliamentary Debates, Vols. xxxi. and xxxiii., Sir Robert Peel's Speech on Motion for a Committee, April 3, 1816.] "These were strong words from a master manufacturer," says the Duke of Argyll, writing in 1866, "but they were not more strong than true."

It is of high interest to notice that almost precisely one hundred years ago, the cotton factory system, on account of new mechanical inventions, was passing through a great transition exceedingly similar to that which the shoe factory system is now passing from the same cause. One hundred years ago this year, Sir Richard Arkwright perfected that marvelous combination of mechanical adjustments known as the spinning frame. Hargreaves' great invention of the spinning jenny took place in 1765. And Crompton's celebrated combination, in the mule jenny of the two preceding machines, followed in 1787. In strict analogy with what is now passing before our eyes in the history of a great sister industry, the invention of new machinery in the cotton manufacture revolutionized its processes; and the invention of one important machine necessitated the invention of others.

But the steam engine had not yet appeared. A factory system therefore sprung up in connection with vast establishments located on streams. Of necessity, the sites chosen were, in a majority of instances, at a distance from preexisting towns and in thinly populated districts. In order to secure permanent labor, a system of apprenticeship was adopted, by which operatives were bound to work for a definite period. The consequences of congregated labor under no regulation except the unrestrained competition of manufacturers, began to appear.

---

*Cook was educated in the traditional fashion and like many of his peers looked to Europe, especially England and Germany, for intellectual anchors. Many intellectuals of the post-Civil-War period suffered from Anglophilism and an infatuation with German intellectual developments. Ironically, like most Americans, Cook saw the textile district of Lancastershire as the prime example of the evils of industrialization, although by 1870 Fall River, Massachusetts (just seventy miles south of Lynn), was a textile town which most Englishmen felt was as bad as or worse than Lancastershire. See John Cumbler, *Working Class Community in Industrial America* (Westport, Conn.:Greenwood Press, 1979), and "Transatlantic Working Class Institutions," *Journal of Historical Geography*, Vol. 63 (1980): 275–290.

Hardly more frightful abuses have sprung up under the factory system outside of large towns. A whole generation of boys and girls and youths and men and women of all ages, says one of the most considerate of historians, "were growing up under conditions of physical degeneracy, of mental ignorance, and of moral corruption." The very title of the bill by which Sir Robert Peel began, in 1802, the great series of the English Parliamentary Acts in promotion of factory reform was, "For the preservation of the health and morals of apprentices and others employed in the cotton and other mills, and in cotton and other factories." The health and morals! Upon these points all the vast mass of English factory legislation turns to the present moment. It is significant to notice that when congregated labor under the factory system was tried for half a century in England at a distance from large towns, it exhibited, taken by itself and aside from any now outgrown evils of the plan of apprenticeship, a tendency to perils and abuses such as to call for the most decisive parliamentary interference.

The new star of the steam engine blazed across the mechanical sky; took a fixed place in it; and immediately there was a new grouping of constellations. The vast manufacturing establishments which existed at a distance from towns were transferred to crowded populations. Between 1802 and 1815, the factory system was transformed into its present shape. It was the birth of the inventions of Hargreaves and Arkwright and Crompton and Watt. It was a system wholly new in the world. Immediately, a tendency to perils and abuses appeared which called for vigorous parliamentary repression. English Parliaments have not been remarkable for unnecessary interference with trade, nor for sentimental legislation. The larger part of the manufacturing wealth of the kingdom was thrown into the scale against factory reform. But the cause of that reform has steadily advanced because Parliament has been forced by the terrible revelations of its own commissions of factory inquiry, again and again to interfere. The moral and industrial perils of congregated labor under the factory system in large towns! It was thought that the tendency of the factory system to these perils was corrected by the great Factory Act of 1833. Eleven years passed. The Factory Regulation Act of 1844 was found necessary. Two years insued. Interference, always unwelcome to Parliament and always against some of the deepest traditions of English law, was found needful in spite of previous interference. In 1847 the celebrated Ten Hours Act was passed. Experience continues to teach. In 1853, the Childrens' Labor Act is found indispensable. Against every one of these great measures, the larger part of the leading manufacturers threw their heaviest influence. I recite before this assembly the list of the great Acts of factory reform wrung from Parliament, in Great Britain, to prove the inherent tendencies of congregated labor under the factory system in large towns to moral and industrial perils and abuses. A board of factory inspectors, with ample powers, sits to-day in London, with subordinate inspectors in various districts making reports to the central officers weekly. The number of prosecutions and informations instituted by the inspectors under the factory acts from 1836 to 1854, was 3696. [Encyclopedia Britannica, Eighth Edition, Vol. xxi., p. 791.]

This is the historical reputation of that system of congregated labor in large towns into which the largest trade of the United States is now inevitably passing.

Large Floating Populations of Towns Engaged in the Fluctuating Industries.

Ominous enough in itself, this fact is yet more ominous from the most important circumstance that this vast branch of manufactures belongs to the fluctuating rather than to the uninterrupted industries; and must, on that account, give rise in large towns to large fluctuating populations. The perils of congregated labor in large towns are large enough; but the perils of congregated labor in large towns with large floating populations have an established name that makes it impossible to speak too strongly of the worth of family life as a moral police in society.

He who comes home at night to a circle that know him well and watch his daily course, has a kind of daily appearance to make before a moral tribunal. The bliss of the home affections is a shield from vice, not only because it is bliss, but because it makes any conduct that needs concealment from the moral tribunal of the most intimate circle as painful as the bliss of ingenuousness and trust is great.

From side to side of the globe every place where a large floating population congregates is found to be a stormy moral coast. In face of universal experience I need not pause to prove the moral perils of homelessness. Those centres in New England where large floating populations gather will always be found to exhibit peculiar moral perils.

All the more to be honored and trusted for their endurance of the breakers, is that percentage of most worthy people to be found in every floating population. Not only am I aware of the existence of hundreds of excellent people in floating populations, but also of the duty of receiving these with especial cordiality to our hearts and homes. But in a large town, there is in a floating population not only an intermixture of the thoughtless and giddy and falling, but, further down, and most to be feared, a percentage of the thoroughly bad. Men and women who have the worst of reasons for leading a floating life need not be many in any floating population to do immense mischief. New England is not so saintly in her cities that she can afford to forget that the exigencies of trade and the wonderful growth of means of intercommunication, have brought into some of her inland large towns evils thoroughly analogous to the old and traditional evils of seaports. All kinds of people gather in a floating population. In a large city, in a floating population, it is not incautious to ask, not every tenth man, but every tenth man who pretends to a peculiar interest in your affairs, Have you ever been in jail? Every great city is a collection of camps. He who knows one stratum of the society only, does not know the city. He who knows dissipated Paris does not know Paris, but only a particular camp in Paris. So of New York and London and Berlin, and every lesser town in its proportion. The moral perils of homelessness added to the perils of this bad percentage from outside, put the solemn duty upon the resident population of these stormy moral coasts to throw the moral lighthouses of church, library, and school, but especially the lighthouses of right industrial arrangements, far out upon the edges of the reefs.

But, besides the operation of the fluctuating character of the shoe trade to produce large floating populations in large towns devoted to that trade, another cause operating to the same end exists in the great subdivision of labor which the new system of the industry has introduced. A person arrives here fresh from a New Hampshire farm and never having seen a factory. It is possible for him to be taught in a very few days to perform some one of the simpler parts of the work. I have seen in the factories machines which I think I could myself be taught in three days how to feed. The result of all this is, that in the two brisk periods of your year, among the thousands who come here, there are some hundreds who expect to learn their parts on arriving. I call attention to the fact that in the new system of the trade, there are many branches of work into and out of which a man can float, without floating in and out through the gate of an apprenticeship of seven years.

So important in this city is the distinction between the floating and the resident population, that you will allow me to use the phrase floating Lynn to characterize the former, and old Lynn to describe the latter. In the fifteen thousand now employed here in your chief industry, which is advancing so rapidly in size, there is already a population of five or seven thousand, who are here or not here, according as your business is at its points of greatest or least activity. I speak tonight with the question constantly in my mind how large that floating population is to be in ten years, in twenty, in fifty, or a hundred, in this city, in Haverhill, in New England as a whole, in New York, and in Philadelphia.

Cautions in Respect to the Discussion.

The hour that is passing before this assembly is a serious one, for we are called now, in the face of these five considerations, to study our duty in respect to the special measures of prevention and reform, which are required by the solemn and multitudinous voices of local and national interests concerned in the perils which history and the most recent experience point out as undeniably involved in the very nature of the largest trade of the United States.

It is little for me to say, speaking on a theme like this, that I will not be the instrument of the capitalists. I will not be the instrument of the manufacturers. I will not be the instrument of the Crispin Lodges.* I will not be the instrument of the parlors of any church. I will speak tonight in no sense as the apologist of this class or that. The theme is too serious for partisanship, or for the concealment of truth.

Let me say also that I have not suffered myself to take up a theme so complicated and weighty without an extended and most serious attention to it, not as exhibited in books merely, but as seen in the swarming life of this city; not as seen in the opinions of this class of men or of that, but as seen by men who have the most different interests involved concerning it, and the most widely separated points of view. I have been through more than a few of your factories. I have conversed with a large number of your leading manufacturers. I have consulted carefully with many working men.

You will not always allow yourselves to be confused by the criticism I make on floating Lynn, which I have already distinguished from the resident population of the city.

The chief proposition I defend is that the working class of the manufacturing centres of New England have a right to ask of the

*Labor unions of shoe workers, very active in Lynn during the period of Cook's lectures.

employing class, that the moral perils of the work-rooms under the factory system, shall be made, for themselves and for their children, as few and small as possible.*

Foul and Clean Systems of Work-Room Management.

There is a foul and there is a clean system of workroom management in shoe factories. To speak at once to the point, there are workrooms in this city, in which men and women, boys and girls, gathered in large part at random out of a floating population, are sandwiched together like herrings in a box, and, uninterrupted by the noise of machinery, it is not infrequently foul talk, profanity, and tobacco smoke from morning to night! I am not speaking of cotton factories, in which the noise of machinery prevents free conversation between operatives, and in which I should not call for a separation of the sexes in the workrooms. But in shoe factories it is notoriously easy for a few foul mouths, not hard to be found in a floating population, to corrupt a whole room. This herring-box system I call a foul system. (Applause.) I ask you and I beg the general public to notice that I am venturing all these assertions before a crowded audience which understands better than any other audience in New England, the facts of which I speak. There is not the slightest business necessity for mingling the sexes in the workrooms. But, besides seeing the sexes of about the same numbers in closely packed rooms, I have sometimes seen four or five young women crowded into the same room with twenty-five or thirty men; or three working thus; or two; or one. I do not assert that a majority of mouths are foul in the factories; but I deliberately make myself responsible for the public assertion that a father who wishes the welfare of his daughter cannot be expected to put her into factory life in a large proportion of the workrooms of this city. There is no saying more common here than that a father does not like to put his daughter or son into many of the factories. The common and permanent opinion as to what the answer would be to the question, Would you put your own daughter into workrooms managed on such a system? is a test of the character of that system. A management in respect of which the answer to this question is notoriously and always No, I call a foul system. Perhaps I have put more than a hundred times this question, or its equivalent, and have been answered invariably in exactly these words, or their equivalent:

*Thus labor loses the right to influence conditions of labor but is granted the right to influence of environment.

"Before putting my daughter into workrooms managed on that system, I would see her, in some other place, work her fingers to the bone!" This is a terrible condemnation of a system wholly unnecessary in itself; affecting, here and elsewhere, a vast operative population, and likely to affect a population larger and larger.* (Applause.)

On the other hand, as the example of five or six of the largest factories here abundantly proves, there is a clean system of workroom management in shoe towns. In one of the largest factories of this city I have seen the sexes in separate rooms everywhere from basement to roof. Where this arrangement is made and care is taken to appoint men, of irreproachable character to oversee the workrooms of the men, and women of irreproachable character to oversee the work-rooms of the women, the answer to the test question is different. I have information as to single rooms in this city in which there is every reason to believe the moral condition is good because care has been taken as to the moral character of overseers; and, as to others, in which there is every reason to believe the moral character is bad, because there has been carelessness as to the moral character of overseers.

When the character of a floating population, the effect of the floating on the resident population, the inflamability of human nature, the immense numbers likely to be affected by the varied influences of the workroom arrangements, are kept in view, all that can be said in respect to the foul system is simply that capitalists and manufacturers ought to have sense enough not to adopt it. One hardly feels like offering arguments in the case. It is, however, as a temporary arrangement, though not as a permanent, slightly cheaper to manage on the careless system than on the careful. There is, too, now and then a man of theory, or some

"Lily-handed, snow-banded, dilettante"

critic knowing nothing of manufactures, who, overlooking the immense distinctions between the influences of the sexes on each other in the parlors of good society, or in a high school, for example, and their influences on each other in these rooms, filled from a floating population without any careful sifting of characters at the doors, judges on general principles, without having examined the case in actual life, that the mingling of the sexes in these workrooms from morning to night

*Despite Cook's paternalistic view of the world, most families did feel a necessity to put their daughters into the factories, and it is questionable whether or not it was a father's decision.

may be an excellent thing. And there are others who judging from exceptional instance or instances, where the character of those engaged in particular rooms has been particularly good, and the overseers men of irreproachable character, and the sexes mingled to apparent advantage, think that this is the best general rule for the large, floating populations of the manufacturing centres of this trade, present and future in New England and elsewhere. I fully admit the existence of such exceptions. No one is prouder than I am of the record of the Lowell factory girls in publishing the celebrated Lowell Offering, made up exclusively of their own contributions. There are, to my personal knowledge, workrooms in this city which may rank in every respect with those from which this paper was issued. But it is amazing that any man should forget the immense changes in the general character of our operative populations in the last twenty-five years. It is possible that there is a man in this audience into whose ears it never has been whispered that the operative populations in New England are not quite what they were twenty years ago? The suspension of the Lowell Offering in 1848 marks the beginning of a change which has not left behind it the hope that such publications will be numerous in the future. All these facts are matters of public notoriety, and not to be answered by the recitation of any score of exceptional cases.*

For the sake, therefore, of any who have judged the matter at a distance, or from exceptional cases, I purpose to name a few arguments not needed by any man who will examine the theme close at hand, or by a wide induction of instances.

Arguments Against the Foul System.

As definitions, let me state, once for all, that by the foul system I mean the mingling of the sexes in the workrooms, and carelessness as to the moral character of overseers; and by the clean system, the separation of the sexes in the workrooms, and carefulness as to the moral character of overseers. My main assertion is that the moral perils of the latter system are less than those of the former. By workrooms, I mean the rooms which may be strictly so called. Of course I have no objection to lady book-keepers: they are usually more steady than young men. Nor have I objection to female help in the packing rooms. In these the proprietors themselves are usually present.

*The "whispered" change Cook alludes to here is the increase in foreign-born operatives, particularly Irish, in the textile mills of Lowell and Lawrence. He is hinting here at "ethnic inferiority" of the Irish.

I shall give ten reasons for two special measures, the separation of the sexes in the workrooms and carefulness as to the moral character of overseers: ten reasons for two things; and as I beg you to notice, for the one measure as much as for the other.

The Door of Entrance to the Workrooms, Not a Sieve.

1. The chances in the shoe trade in any large town are extraordinarily great that bad men and bad women will occasionally be found in the workrooms; and these chances arise from the five circumstances, (1) That the door of entrance to the workrooms is not, and, on account of the number of changeable operatives, is not likely soon to be made, a moral sifting machine; (2) That the industry has each year two brisk and often painfully hurried periods, and two of comparative inactivity; (3) That the percentage of operatives changeable within the year is large on account of the fluctuations, and is estimated here to be thirty-three per cent of the whole number; (4) That, on account of the fluctuations of the industry, the floating population of shoe towns is likely to be large, and it is out of this population, itself not sifted, that operatives, in the hurried periods of the work, are taken into the workrooms through a door that is not a sieve; (5) That it is notorious that in the exigencies of the trade in the greatly hurried seasons, operatives that are expert are often retained for their expertness without any high degree of caution as to their moral character.

Such, in a large town, is the very structure of this branch of manufactures. The very nature of the industry points by all these five arguments to the necessity of a separation of the sexes in the workrooms, and carefulness as to the moral character of overseers. If there is a business necessity for packing inks and silks together, it is business sagacity to pack them as separate parcels.

All the factory streets of this city just now blossom with advertising boards for operatives. A strip of lasting board is put out at the door or window of an establishment with the words on it: "Heelers wanted"; "Stitchers wanted"; or, "Binders wanted". At two periods of the year these lasting boards are one of the most characteristic sights in your city. You know perfect well that, when work is greatly hurried, the first workman that comes that is skillful is likely to be taken for the time. At Lawrence and Lowell operatives are engaged, in a majority of cases, by the year. They sign formal regulations on entering a factory.* Neither

*Cook's reference to the positive aspect of this habit of forcing operatives to sign "yellow dog" contracts indicates his authoritarian model.

of these customs exists here. The first argument for the separation of the sexes and the appointment of only men of irreproachable character as overseers in the workrooms is, that the lasting board is not a sieve.

Opinions of Resident Physicians

2. Allow me to say that there is no class of men whose opinions I respect more highly in regard to the real inner life of cities, than I do that of such physicians as combine among their qualifications scholarship, experience, ability, and candor.* It does no harm for the student of the moral condition of cities to ask questions of such men. While I continue to be such a student, I shall keep my ears open to this testimony, if my ears are not long ears.

I have put behind me all that I have now said from the beginning, in order that I might fitly, as I now may, state the decisive argument that physicians in this city, resident here for a long period, and combining the qualifications of scholarship, ability, and candor, lay at the door of the new factory system, or want of system, a startling increase of vice in the floating population. It is, of course, difficult to make estimates on such a subject. Even when they are numerous enough to nibble at any careless feet on the pavement, and to rustle now and then in the outer walls of private homes and of churches, as God grant they may never be here, there is no census taken of gutter rats. He is somewhat more than simple who looks at the police record for a complete account of all that passes in a large town. The most solemn public responsibilities make it my duty to know this city thoroughly. There is one question which tests the secret trend of under currents in a crowded population very well; and that question I have put. Of a physician having all the qualifications I have named, I asked what in his judgment had been the growth of the worst vices here in the last ten years, as tested by their physical penalities coming under medical observation. In two conversations, he told me that his judgment was, that, in the floating population of this city, the infamous diseases had increased ten per cent in ten years in proportion to the population!† I was moved as if smitten by an electric bolt. He adhered to his opinion; and, after making all allowance for the war, and every other cause, laid the horrible blame upon the mingling of the

*Physicians as professionals epitomize the middle class that Cook is appealing to.

†By "infamous diseases" Cook means venereal disease. Venereal disease was a common fear and signpost for moral reformers of the Victorian period. It was often used by both moral reformers and health reformers as a fear tactic to rally support for reform. It also raised the purient interest of the audience and was a surrogate for reference to sexual intercourse itself. This was always useful for spicing up a lecture.

sexes in the new factory system of this city. I thought the opinion worth testing by inquiry. I wished to see whether others agreed with it. You will notice that it referred to floating Lynn, and by no means to the resident population. Riding, soon after I received this opinion, with two men advanced in years, but of excellent ability and who had known the city intimately from their boyhood, I quoted the opinion and asked their judgment as to it. They both said, without hesitation, that they should not wonder if the opinion were just, such were the moral perils of a large floating population. I had occasion not long after to call at the office of a gentleman whose public position gives him an excellent knowledge of the city and especially of the wants of the working people. I mentioned the estimate to him. He said at once that it was not too high, and perhaps not high enough. A group of gentlemen who sat by seemed to give a general assent to his opinion. Startled beyond measure, I selected a second physician whom I considered the equal of any other in the city in the four qualifications I have named, a man whose balance of mind you all honor, but whom I must not more particularly describe; and, calling on him one evening, was most cordially received. I simply said that I was investigating the moral condition of the city; that I valued the aid of a physician's judgment; and that such and such an opinion had been given to me, mentioning both the estimate I have already quoted, and the name of its author, though saying nothing whatever of the factories. "The estimate is not high enough," was the reply. "Since the sexes have been mingled in the new system of the factories, the floating population has shown the effect. And what less could be expected? Twenty-five or thirty by fifteen or twenty feet in size with a dozen men and a dozen women, and boys and girls into the same room let tobacco smoke, and profanity, and foul talk take their course. The estimate is not extravagant, if it is high enough, in respect to the effect on the floating population of the mingling of the sexes in the factories." Before this opinion was given, not only had I myself not said a word of the new system; but, so far as I am aware, the physician was not informed from any other resource that I was at all interested in the topic. The reference to the factories on the part of this able physician was wholly gratuitous and unprompted. "But," said I, "what is the effect on the resident population of these perils in the floating? It is hard to make an estimate; but, at Nahant, the people tell me that, after a storm, it is necessary to wash slight salt stains from their windows so much of the spray is blown across the peninsula. Does this floating Lynn, foaming against the resident population, dash any spray over it?" "The figure is a very good one," said the physician: "two percent of the resident population may be injured."* I afterwards consulted carefully with a third medical authority, having all the qualifications; and he endorsed fully, and with minute details of facts, the opinions of the other two, both as to the extent of the evil as to its cause!

3. With the eyes with which you are looking into my face at this moment, I need only to name, as a third argument, the possible future effect of the floating population on the resident, when the former is larger. When the operative's fever broke out into the middle classes in Old England under the old factory system, Robert Peel led a reform; and the abuses in the mills that had been overlooked while only the operatives suffered, were remedied almost exclusively from fear of contagion in other classes.

4. Nor do I need do more than name, after this apalling testimony, the topic of foul mouths in factories.

5. It is plainly impossible to make a proper provision against these evils by either of the two measures taken without the other. Some two or three months since, I visited a factory room on special invitation. The person who invited me and who showed me the room, had spoken of one young woman in it as an exception to the rest, and as resisting every unhealthful moral influence. But he told me that at a previous time the room had been so remarkable for foul talk that no young man could work there any long period and retain his virtue, the girls were so bad. I saw a room some seventy by twenty feet in size; and several young men in one end and young women in the other; cutters and stitchers; no connection of their work requiring that it should be in the same place. When in the room I asked my informant if a particular one of the young women was not the exception of which he had spoken. My informant said she was. The others were course looking. I instance this case in order to add that in any room arranged as that was, even if Washington or Lincoln were overseer, he could not prevent the moral condition from being unhealthful if the character of those in the room should happen to be bad; nor, on the latter supposition, would separate rooms without good overseers be enough. Neither of the two measures will be found sufficient alone to meet the exigencies of manufacturing centres.

6. It is found by experience that it is in the workrooms that a young woman coming here and not resisting, as, thank God, hundreds and thousands do resist, the morally unhealthful influences, loses that natural shyness and modesty which are her charm, and gradually

*Here Cook implies that an increase in venereal disease among workers can spread to the middle class through the patronage of prostitutes by husbands.

acquires a repulsive boldness. There are spiritual and physical signs for every vice. The loss of spiritual shyness and nobleness can be seen, as well as the loss of natural freshness of complexion and of a lustreful flash of the eye. Suppose that a young woman coming here for the first time falls into both an ill-regulated boarding-house and a room of unhealthful moral conditions in a factory. Which will do the more harm? Which will begin the harm? Where will the first indentation of ill occur? Evidently she can choose her companions to a great extent in the boarding-house; and, if she is of high principle, will choose the best she can. But she cannot choose her company in the workroom. She must breathe the atmosphere of the company in the latter eight or ten hours a day. She may, in a large measure, choose her own company in the former, except for perhaps an hour a day. Further on in the history of deterioration, the irregulated boarding-house and the street school may strip the flesh from the peach, but the down of the peach was brushed away in the workrooms. This is found to be the history of the case in tracing almost any individual example of deterioration.

7. It is plain that neither boarding-houses nor churches can do as much for a floating as for a resident population. If the floating population of this city had homes here, I have no doubt it would be as free from moral perils as any population of its size. Not only have they no homes, but they often have difficulty in finding boarding-houses under the best management. No system of corporation boarding-houses, such as exists in the cotton towns, exists here, chiefly because the occupants would most of them be out of the city three months in every twelve.* In a large town devoted to your branch of industry, many things cannot be done by boarding-houses and churches which can be done in a cotton town; and, on this account, what can be done by right industrial arrangements is of all the more urgent importance.

8. I feel it a descent to mention any financial argument; but, if any business man doubts that whatever undermines good order in the working class, also undermines regularity of industry and diminishes the worth of the hours of labor, he need not look far into the history of the factory system to find an opinion not weakened by a doubt.

9. The sentiment of working men and women of the best class is eager and emphatic in favor of the separation of the sexes in shoe factories. I have found this true on all hands in my conversations.

---

*In fact, by the 1870s most corporate boardinghouses were used not to control morals (as theoretically they were in antebellum Lowell), but to control labor: to discourage labor unions and break strikes. See John Cumbler, *Working Class Community in Industrial America* (Westport, Conn.: Greenwood Press, 1979.)

Obviously the working people are, in this matter, not only the chief sufferers. They are also the best informed. The employers of the present day, though they may have had personal experience as workmen under the old system, have usually, if they are past middle life, had none as operatives under the new. It is worth little for an employer to say that he has had thirty or thirty-five years experience in the shoe business. There have been hardly more than ten years experience in the shoe business in its present form. An employer without experience is an operative, and who judges of what happens in his establishment by what occurs in his presence, is not as wise an adviser in this case as the operative. The sentiment of the working men and working women of the best class is the decisive consideration.

10. The sentiment and the practice of capitalists and manufacturers of the best class are to take pains to appoint men of irreproachable character as overseers, and to separate the sexes in the workrooms. On several occasions, after bringing this topic privately to the notice of manufacturers, as I have repeatedly done, I have found them condemning the foul system, although, on account of some temporary inconvenience in the structure of their factories, their own establishments were not yet wholly free from it. In spite of the practice of the majority of the factories of this city, all of perhaps a score of manufacturers to whom I have presented the subject privately, have, except one, unequivocally favored the system of the separation of the sexes. I must not leave the impression that I have addressed you to-night by the prompting of any one, for I have spoken wholly as an independent student and critic of public affairs. Let me state, however, that I shall not soon forget the emphasis with which, at the head-quarters of this industry in Pearl Street, Boston, one of the ablest merchants there, himself owner of large factories and member of a factory firm known and honored throughout Eastern Massachusetts, said to me on my bringing the topic of to-night to his attention, his own practice corresponding with his advice: "Do you adhere to the ground of the separation of the sexes. It is of high public importance. There is not the slightest business reason for mingling the sexes in the new system, and any number of moral and industrial reasons against it."

Why discuss this subject publicly? Because only a powerful public sentiment will correct the evil. In what method will public sentiment aid? It is not difficult to point out the steps. Let it be made socially as unpopular for a man to manage a factory on a careless system and mutilate souls as to manage a railway on a careless system and mutilate bodies. Then the better class of men will be influenced. Let a majority, thus gradually won, set right fashions, and even the moneygripes, and men lower down, will be reached. Business is a regiment. For industrial reasons men must keep step with each other in it. Let a majority of the Board of Trade of any city set right business fashions, and the inferior men who care only for money are usually brought sooner or later to respect the step of the regiment.

Conclusion

I need only to invoke the visible presence before this assembly of the lofty spirits of Sir Robert Peel and Lord Shaftesbury, to suggest sufficiently the historic perils of congregated labor under the factory system in large towns. Would that in the air above every manufacturing centre of New England, Robert Peel and Lord Shaftesbury, colossal and admonitory in archangelic stature, might each stand to teach, with one hand pointing toward Old England and the other stretched as a shield over New England, the methods of avoiding here the perils which have arisen there.

God grant that the day may never come when American society shall be divided into two classes, the unemployed rich and the unemployed poor, the former a handful and the latter a host! To that we shall come, as so many parts of Europe have come already, when our population is as thick as theirs, unless all good men and true unite to keep certain industrial ghosts that now trouble Europe from crossing the Atlantic.

Two great axioms rule modern manufactures. They are, that subdivision of labor increases the skill of the workman: and that, other things being equal, the larger a manufacturing establishment, the greater the profits. These are the organizing laws which explain most of the phenomena of manufacturing populations; and will continue to explain them for ages to come, although it is only in the last age that the laws can be said to have been discovered.

It is the principle of subdivision of labor which confines the modern operative more and more to some single detail, the work upon which, after it becomes a habit, calls into activity only a few of the mental powers; has in it no variety, and so does not develop the mind by tasking it at different points; is in itself of only petty importance, and so excites little enthusiasm in labor and even little pride of skill. De Tocqueville, in a celebrated passage, discussing the modern science of manufacturers, asks what can be expected of the human intelligence, when, year after year to twelve or ten hours a day, it is occupied in the single detail of making heads for pins. [De Tocqueville, Alexis, Democracy in America,

Vol. ii., Book ii., Chap. xx.] The principle of subdivision of labor has an inherent tendency to dwarf the operative mind, unless the most power-ful stimulants are applied outside of factory hours to develop the faculties which the manufacturing work never calls into activity. Out-side of factory hours! Those words are lightly uttered only by the inexperienced in operative life. Outside of factory hours there are, properly speaking, for operative populations tasked ten or twelve hours a day in close apartments, no hours at all. The labor of the mill or of the mine, which goes on in all weathers with the invariability of the sun in its courses, is not to be compared with agricultural labor, inter-rupted by the changes of the seasons and even of the daily sky. Twelve hours or ten in a factory, and then three hours or two enthusiastic pursuit of mental culture! No eyes yet born are destined to see that wonder grow common. There are a few mental and physical constitu-tions vigorous enough to combine these two sets of hours, and so counteract the narrowing mental effect of labor for years at one unvar-ied mechanical detail. But the mass of operative populations can be expected to exhibit no such physical, to say nothing of such mental and moral, vigor. They are swept remorselessly under the wheels of subdi-vision of labor and long hours. In women and children, who constitute nearly half of operative populations, how much life is left for mental culture after twelve hours severe labor in a mill? But subdivision of labor increases skill; increase of skill increases productiveness; increase of productiveness increases profits; and long hours are the scythes that reap the gain. This is the law of manufacturers; and, it is only saying what is evident in the nature of things, and no less evident in the condition of all manufacturing populations where factory occupation has been hereditary for three or four generations, that the tendency of the system is to make the operative class inferior; and the inferior yet more inferior. Emerson stood at the door of the factories of Great Britain and wrote that society is to be admonished of the mischief of the division of labor by the fact that, in three generations, the robust, rural Saxon had degenerated in the mills to the Leicester Stockinger and to the imbecile Manchester Spinner, far on the way to be spiders and needles. [Emerson, R. W., *English Traits*, chap. x.]

On the other hand, the operation of the principle that, other things being equal, the larger manufacturing establishment the greater the profits, tends to call out all the capabilities of the minds that lead and organize in manufacturers. It requires capacity in that class, attracts capacity, and tasks capacity. Men of education are often drawn into manufactures by the allurement of the size of enterprises involved. The tension of mind, and the variety of its applications in the conductor of a large establishment are at all points a contrast with the condition of the mind of the operative.

Inevitably, therefore, as the effect must follow the cause, the system of modern manufactures in large populations tends to produce a superior class and an inferior; and, as years go on and the first effects themselves become causes, to make the superior more superior and the inferior more inferior.* I am not denying the advantages of manufacturing eminence; but stating, as a motive for public caution, what political economists have long acknowledged as the disadvantages of such eminence. Even John Stuart Mill, using England as a lens and putting behind that telescope the best eyes of political economy, writes a deliberate chapter [Mill, John Stuart, *Political Economy*, Book iv., chap. vii.] on the Probable Future of the Laboring Classes, and goes so far as to say that he finds the prospect hopeful only because he expects the whole system of wages to be superseded by that of cooperation. But the system of wages is interwoven with the whole structure of modern life, and does not show a tendency to vanish out of history like a morning cloud. The accumulations of wealth fall chiefly to employers and not to operatives. The distance between the two classes is a result of deep causes arising from the two great laws of the manufacturing system. It is out of these laws that there inevitably originates what has been called, in modern times, a manufacturing aristocracy. De Tocqueville, using this phrase, compares the territorial aristocracy of former ages with the manufacturing aristocracy of to-day; and finds the former superior to the latter because it was bound by law, or thought itself bound by usage, as the latter is not, to come to the relief of its serving men and to succor them in their distresses. [*Democracy in America*, Vol. ii., chap. xx. Also Vol. ii., Book iv., chap.v.] I see no charm in democracy that can alter the nature of things. The subtle laws of subdivision of labor and of size of establishment apply to manufactures in New England as well as in Old England. Under some restraints from the nature of our institutions, they will, notwithstanding, produce here as there an employing class and an operative class; and perpetually tend to make the distance between rich and poor in manufacturing populations wider and wider.

*Cook is articulating here Lysenko's view of environmental heredity. According to Cook the environment creates conditions in people that could become hereditary. Since he saw the factory system as an environment not encouraging independent development, he saw workers becoming degenerate. Thus he was concerned about reform of the environment. Variations on this theme became a central aspect of late-nineteenth-century reform and part of the ideological framework of late-nineteenth-century racism.

De Tocqueville thought that the friends of democracy should keep their eyes anxiously fixed upon the operation of these two laws; and that, if ever a permanent inequality of conditions again penetrated into the world, it might be predicted that this is the gate by which it will enter.

I find a right to speak very plain words in New England, the whole Atlantic slope of which is a factory, by lifting up my hand and pointing to Manchester and Liverpool, to Birmingham and Leeds, and London and Rouen. John Ruskin says that the unemployed poor of Great Britain are daily becoming more violently criminal. A searching distress, he told the University of Oxford last winter, invades the middle classes, arising partly from their vanity in living always up to their incomes, and partly from their folly in imagining that they can subsist in idleness upon usury. [John Ruskin, *Lectures on Art before the University of Oxford*, 1870. p.27.] Factory reform and factory legislation are old and great and grave themes in English literature. They are old and great and grave themes in Parliament. The best mark of himself Thomas Carlyle has made on the face of this planet, and a mark perhaps not soon to be erased, is his discussions of the condition of the working classes as illustrated in the problems relating to the English poor and the questions between capital and labor. Dickens has written more to illustrate this field than any other. Victor Hugo's best words are upon these themes. Romney and Aurora Leigh, in Mrs. Browning's greatest work, are typical characters for the best thought of Europe. Their chief office in the hands of the poetess is to illustrate rival methods in philanthropy toward the working classes. John Bright leads middle England because he teaches the transcendently important truth that, wherever the few live, the nation lives in the cottage. George Peabody endows colleges with his left hand, but with his right builds houses for the London poor, and schoolhouses for the poor of our Southern states. Prince Albert occupied his mature life chiefly by studying the condition of the working classes of London, and particularly the best arrangement for tenement houses. We remember what Alfred Tennyson says of this noblest of the recent English princes:

> Laborious for her people and her poor,
> Voice in the rich dawn of an ampler day,
> Far-sighted summoner of war and waste
> To fruitful strife and revalries of peace.

Let no one be ashamed to discuss the condition of the uncleanest poor. God is what he discussed at Gettysburg and Richmond, at the liberation of the Russian serfs, at the granting of the Magna Charta, at the Restoration of Letters, at the Fall of the Roman empire, at Calvary itself. For two hundred years the most vital causes in politics have turned upon the condition of the many as opposed to the few. It is not likely that it will be different with history for two hundred years to come.

It is most necessary to notice that, on all these themes, the reformers and deformers are yet strangely mingled. The truth that labor reform, both here and in Europe, contains, seems to me, I must confess, a jewel in the coarsest incrustations; and yet no less a jewel for its strange setting. I suppose that the deepest question yet remaining unsolved in this nation is that concerning the relations between capital and labor. Slavery itself was but one form of that question. We hear the retreating footsteps of the discussions concerning slavery, and at the same time the advancing footsteps, under which Europe already shakes, of discussions concerning the working classes in crowded populations. The discontent of the working classes! The discontent of the working classes! This is a sound ominous of much, both good and bad; but it is not the less ominous of the one or of the other for being borne to us on all the four winds of heaven.

In one field of that wide discontent, I have spoken to-night for the largest trade of the United States. I have spoken for Lynn, for Haverhill, for all New England. I have spoken for New York and Philadelphia. Outside of the collieries of Pennsylvania, there is perhaps not a spot on the continent where I could have delivered tonight a speech more needing to be made. Go to the grave of George Peabody, almost in sight of which I speak, and learn your duties to the poor, and toward the present and the future of the vast trade which this city leads. (Applause.)

INTRODUCTION TO LECTURE II

Cook's first lecture stirred tremendous interest in the city of Lynn. Many citizens felt that he was addressing a serious issue of moral concern, while others felt that his lecture was an attack on the good name of the city and many of its inhabitants. Both the floors and galleries of the Music Hall were packed for the second lecture. It was reported that over one thousand persons were turned away. The allegations of immorality and degeneracy were widely publicized in the city in the columns and letters of the papers, and debated in the city's taverns and cafes. The belief that Cook was going to expand upon those earlier comments drew the unprecedented overflow crowd.

*The audience greeted Cook's entrance with loud and uncontrolled applause,
interspersed with some catcalls and hostile heckling. When the demonstration
subsided, Cook continued his discussion of the evils of the factory system, concentrating his attack on the immorality of mingling the sexes. Those who came for
excitement were not disappointed. At the end of Cook's discourse, S. M. Bubier, a
local shoe manufacturer who believed that Cook referred to his own factory,
jumped from his seat and mounted the stage, demanding the right to refute Cook's
attacks on the factory system. Cook, aware of the advantages of controversy, asked
the audience to remain and hear Bubier out. The manufacturer claimed that,
having lived in Lynn for 55 years, he knew the city and the industrial system better
than Cook. He denied that there were any factories such as those Cook described,
and asserted that Cook's previous residence in an insane asylum brought his
whole character into question. Bubier's reference to Cook's mental health brought
the house down: the catcalls, hissing and booing finally forced him off the stage.
Cook, realizing that he had the sympathy of the audience, did not even bother to
refute Bubier, but led the audience directly into the hymn, "Majestic Sweetness
Sits Enthroned."*

2. THE EVILS OF THE FACTORY SYSTEM: THE MINGLING OF THE SEXES

My mood to-night is that of morning on the mountains. I feel like
Bismark [sic] before Paris.*

I had anticipated seven styles of sentiment as to my address of last
Sabbath evening. There are three chief parties interested in the discussion—the employed, the employers, and the churches. Each of these is
to be divided between the offended and the unoffended. There are six
parties. But the seventh is the party of hearsay. It is this last that I
anticipated would have the most wildly inaccurate impressions. It is one
thing to hear a speech, and another to hear of it. It is one thing to hear
with the ears, and another to hear with the elbows. In spite, however, of
all disadvantages, the working men, I am assured on all sides, are with
me, almost to a man.† I have to thank nearly every paper of the city for
a more or less favorable notice of my remarks as a whole. One of them
fully agrees with me as to the moral dangers of the system, or want of

*This remark, which recurs several times in the course of Cook's lectures, refers to
the conquest by Prussia, under Prime Minister Bismarck, of France during the
Franco–Prussian War.

†Although, as we shall see later, the working men were not totally supportive of
Cook, there was substantial support particularly from the old, Protestant, skilled
workers.

system, which I discussed. I find powerful support in the churches.* In estimating public sentiment, the difficulty is, that men in a particular eddy imagine the whole ocean to be moved as their eddy is. It is my duty, as a student of public sentiment, to study all the eddies. I am assured (though I do not lean on the assurance), and assured from many very differently prejudiced authorities, that the capitalists and employers are with me, except five or six, who are very angry. I know, beyond all question, by their personal testimony to me, that every manufacturer of the many with whom I have conversed, with the exception of one, is in favor of the two measures I recommended—*the separation of the sexes in the workrooms, and the appointment of good moral men as overseers.* In view of the wildness of the statements on which the party of hearsay have formed their opinions, I think it not useless to remark that what the audience said here last Sabbath evening is, as an indication of public sentiment, not wholly unimportant. Three times during the address, and again at its close, the audience, in spite of its being Sabbath, and the place one used for the time as a church, gave open applause in a marked way. The audience—which represented excellently the whole city—meant to approve the general drift.

Certain statements which I made privately in the confidence of my own parlor, have been thrust before the public in a childish card. If any one thinks that this is large and dignified business, the opinion must stand on its own merits. *I call public attention to the fact, that it was not by means of anything I said publicly that any allusion of mine in a public way was brought down to the low arena of personality.* I referred to a room about seventy feet long and twenty wide. I suppose there may be twenty or fifty such in Lynn. I have myself seen several; and it is my conviction that in some of these the moral conditions were bad, and that the moral dangers of the arrangements unnecessarily adopted by the employers were great. *I could easily have chosen illustrations elsewhere, under evidence of a different character, and fit to bear the severest tests.* I suppose that all in Lynn who have given any thorough attention to the subject know this; and the working men best of all. Of course, there are most excellent factory rooms in this city, and most excellent people in them. I could point out other rooms in Lynn where these moral dangers do not exist, or exist to a vastly less extent, and this on account of other arrangements adopted by the employers. There is a foul and there is a clean system in this largest trade of the United States; and I stand for the latter, and have defined what I mean by the former and the latter.

*Note the exception of the Catholic Church as expressed at pages 227–230.

I do not know that any one has assailed, or attempted to assail, my chief assertion, *that the moral dangers of the latter system are less than those of the former.* The working men and working women cry out for the clean system. God hear their cry! I am their friend, and the friend of this city, and the friend of other cities having similar interests, by giving this cry utterance; and in doing so at a particular juncture, when the whole vast trade throughout the United States is, on account of the invention of new machinery, in a state of transition, and is adopting a system likely to be a precedent for five hundred years.*

Old Lynn I have always distinguished from floating Lynn. I have repeatedly said that I am proud of old Lynn, although I have pointed out its dangers from floating Lynn, on account of this transition state of the great branch of industry which employs here, directly or indirectly, ten or fifteen thousand people, and for the last ten years has put this city at the head of a trade larger than the coal, the iron, or the cotton, and made the fashions it shall set for that great public interest of altogether more than local importance. Instead of the few times I have publicly touched this theme, I should have been justified, by its local, as well as by its general, importance, in touching it oftener; but, in the few times I have touched it, I have most carefully avoided every statement that could endanger the effect of calm, guarded, and dispassionate public discussion by a pitiful descent to personalities about names and places.

The bondage of the pulpit is a theme in the thoughts of many, and on the lips of but a few. I do not consider myself at liberty to allow this occasion to pass without inculcating, for the honor of the church which I represent (and it is highly to its honor), for the honor of this city, and for the public good, the lesson that, Wendell Phillips† is inaccurate when he sneers at the pulpits for being turned by the great wheel of the factories. This is an important public lesson; and I have friends watching me from near and from far who would never forgive me if I failed to use this occasion to utter this grave and perfectly frank word on a theme of such grave public significance. *It is really of public importance that it should be taught in some manufacturing centre of New England, and here and now as well as anywhere, that, while the envy of the rich by the poor is to be*

---

*Cook was well aware of not only the early industrial structure in the shoe industry, but the likelihood that this mode of production would become the pattern for the rest of the nation. It was this awareness that gave him his sense of urgency for reform.

†Wendell Phillips was an important mid-nineteenth-century Boston reformer who was an ardent abolitionist and leader of the American Anti-Slavery Society. After the Civil War, Phillips turned to other reforms, particularly women's rights, support of labor unions, and regulation of corporations.

abhorred and the benefactions of the rich to the church are to be eulogized, no gold-dust is to be allowed to choke, or to bring hesitation or quaver, in the pulpit, to the clear bugle-note of truth.* The clear bugle-note of truth, I say. I mean calm, clear, dispassionate, unselfish, guarded discussion, not of what is most popular, but of what most needs to be said, even if it be a chief sin of poor against rich, or of rich against poor. The hopes of rich and poor train behind that bugle-note. I had rather my lips should be closed forever than that, on the Lord's day, in God's house, any hesitation or quaver should come into that note, with the bugle at my lips, toss into it gold-dust what hand or hands will or can. If I had any other spirit, I should be obliged to read in a sense of the profoundest irony, not intended by Mrs. Browning, her words:

> Now press the clarion on thy *woman's* lips,
> (Love's holy kiss shall still keep consecrate,)
> And breathe the fine, keen breath along the brass,
> And blow all class walls level as Jericho's
> Past Jordan; crying from the top of souls
> To souls that here assembled on earth's flats,
> To get them to some purer eminence
> Than any hitherto beheld for clouds—
> What height we know not, but the way we know.

I had rather be any other kind of spaniel than a pulpit spaniel. If any one has mistaken me, while yet a young man, for a member of that rare species, I must remark that I hope the race is becoming extent in New England, even in the manufacturing centres, where the distinctions between rich and poor are perhaps the widest. I may not know myself; but I do not think I am a being capable of being wrapped up in the soft, sweet-scented paper of social obligations, and put into a rich man's waistcoat pocket (or a poor man's either, for that matter, though I had much rather be in the latter than in the former)†. Much less am I capable of being put into the coarse paper of dictatorial and excited language, with its rough shards of inaccurate statement, inuendo, evasion, personality, and browbeating, and thrust bodily into such pocket; or pinned in, with any bar of gold, however large. I make no charges against any man. I do not refer at all to the past. I refer only to the future. But I say that if (I beg you to notice that I say *if*) any two, or

---

*Cook is here articulating a neutralist position for the church in the conflict between labor and capital, which became the hallmark of the conservative wing of the social gospel movement.

†Again, the social gospel theme.

three, or ten, or any other number of rich men think they own the pulpits of this manufacturing centre, I must say that for this property the great seal of the Lord the King is not on their title-deeds.

Every man to me is just as large as his capacity, his training, his conscientiousness, and his attention to the subject in hand. Take out either of these four qualifications, and the rest, however large, no matter what wealth or office adds, are not large enough to make a man large. Every man to me is just as large as his reasons. I purpose to continue perfectly open, calm, independent, guarded, public speech, with no other rules to guide me in doing so in making social distinctions, besides these.

Introduction to Lecture 3

Once again Cook filled the Music Hall to capacity. The storm of letters, both pro and con, that continued to fill the local papers guaranteed him an attentive audience, which "anticipat[ed] that the subject which he ha[d] agitated the community to such an extent within the past few weeks would again be reverted to by Rev. Cook."[70] Cook did refer to his earlier controversy, again raising the problem of the floating population and the dangers it posed for social control. But he spent most of the third talk on new areas of concern about the factory system. Cook took the mill towns of Lowell and Lawrence as models of the way an ordered society should be run in the new industrial era. In doing so he looked at Lowell and Lawrence from the perspective of half a century earlier. (See Appendix A for a full discussion of the mill towns and the conflict between their image as industrial arcadias and their reality as oppressive industrial cities.)

In keeping with his original idea of social reform, Cook also addressed the issue of child labor, long an issue of concern in Massachusetts. In the late 1840s, the New England Workingmen's Association and the Female Labor Reform Association of women textile workers demanded an end to child labor and linked the limitation of child labor with their petition campaign for shorter hours. In 1848 New Hampshire limited child labor and in 1849 Maine joined the Granite State. In 1852 Ohio outlawed employment of children under age fourteen in factories, and Massachusetts passed a series of bills designed to limit child labor. Unfortunately, most of the bills passed by these states were either ineffective or not enforced. The Reverend Joseph Cook, in 1871, did not go so far as to support limitation on child labor, but rather argued for the maintenance of a moral environment in the factory. He thus moved further away from a direct attack on the manufacturers' practices and closer toward the issue of moral reform of the workers themselves. He admitted the right of workers to make demands on their employers, but limited these demands to the issue of moral environment. He did not raise the issue whether the workers have a right to demand safe conditions or adequate wages for adults, such that child labor could be avoided.

3. THE ISSUE OF CHILD LABOR

Henry IV of France once said, and the remark had been gratefully remembered for two hundred years, that he hoped the day would come when every working man in his kingdom might have, as often as he pleased, a chicken for dinner. If there is a political ruler in the civilized part of the world who would not say this now, he is as much an exception to the drift of the age, and to the tendencies of history for the last two hundred years, as the Gulf Stream is an exception in the general drift of the Atlantic. But when Henry IV said this, the speech was a singular one for a great ruler to make. Everything in history for two hundred years illustrates God's pity for the poor. De Tocqueville said that he regarded the progress of the democratic principle in governments as a providential fact—the result of a divine decree. It was universal. It was enduring. It was irresistible. All men and all events contributed to this progress. He found in it the sacred characters of a providential fact, and he stood in awe before it. But this progress is only one illustration of God's pity for the poor. The day has come for nearly the whole world that can be called civilized, when to say what Henry IV said is to say nothing singular.

Tell working men and working women what you please, you cannot make them believe that he is not their friend who is the friend of their children. I have undertaken to maintain before you that the working men and working women of the manufacturing centres of New England have a right to ask of the capitalists and employers of those centres, that when the working people put their children into the workshops, where they must earn their support by daily manual toil from morning to night, the arrangements of those workrooms shall be such that the moral danger to their children shall be as little as possible. This is the outline of all I have said. *The working class have a right to ask this of the employing class.*

In putting before you this assertion, I do not regard myself as saying anything off the line of the speech of Henry IV. I do not consider myself as given to enthusiastic speech; for I hope there is something of caution in my nature, as well as of impetuosity. But if there is any line of thought on which I might throw away all my caution, and give full rein to impetuosity, it is the line of God's pity for the poor. And on precisely that line lies all I have said of the right of the working class in our manufacturing centres to ask of their employers such factory arrangements as shall make the moral temptations of their children as few as possible.

I wish to introduce before you a great and grave theme to-night, and had intended to refer to no other; but in order that I may introduce this other theme with the best effect, it is absolutely necessary for me to brush aside a little mist that lies between your eyes and mine. Fifteen or a score of lies yet walk about the streets; and, in order to get audience for a great theme of another kind here to-night, I must say something to prevent their tramplings being heard in Music Hall.

Six important points are to be kept in the foreground, so far as I have part in the discussion now agitating this city. I am anxious to put principles in the foreground and personalities in the background. These latter have had a ludicrous prominence in certain quarters for the last six days. Rufus Choate and Daniel Webster were once opposed in a legal case that turned on the size of certain wheels, and Webster had the wheels brought into court. When Choate had gone through an elaborate argument to prove that the wheels were not this or that, Webster's only reply was: "Gentlemen, there are the wheels." I wish to keep the great points prominent in the discussion which now has the ear of this city. The facts which I discuss lie close at hand. The wheels are in court.

1. *The lasting-board is not a sieve.* The door through which operatives in the factories of a great town like this are engaged is not a moral sifting-machine. The advertising board is put out at the door or window of a factory, asking for operatives for this class of work or that. In most factories, in the two great brisk seasons of work, whoever comes first that is skilful is likely to be taken. Orders must be filled. Teams must be made up. The operative here signs no regulations, as the operative at a Lawrence or a Lowell cottonmill does.* This is a most important peculiarity of a shoe town, as compared with a cotton town; and, on account of the two circumstances I am about to mention—the periodical lulls in the activity of the shoe factories and the large percentage of changeable operatives—it is difficult to introduce into the shoe factory system the admirable method of sifting operatives according to characters that has long been practiced in the cotton factory system,† which

*See Appendix A.

†In fact, the sifting Cook refers to here was designed to keep trade unionists out—not to maintain a moral character.

does not have to meet the exigencies of such lulls and such a percentage of changeable operatives. A study of the subject at a distance might lead to the opinion that a shoe town and a cotton town are much alike; but the reverse is true. Each has a set of exigencies of its own; and mistakes on the whole subject of the shoe factory system arise from nothing oftener than from the false notion that a shoe town and a cotton town are parallels at most points. The sifting of character at the door of entrance of the workrooms of the factories of a city like this is not, and is not likely to be, by any means microscopic; and this is my first reason for the separation of the sexes and the appointment of good moral men as overseers in the workrooms.

2. *In the shoe trade there are in each year two lulls, each of about a month's duration, and thousands of operatives are dismissed from work in these inactive seasons.* This makes the operative population of a city like this, of necessity, more floating than that of one given to the cotton trade. These lulls do not occur in the coal, the iron, the woolen, or the cotton trade. They are a peculiarity of the shoe trade; and the very best authorities I have consulted among the leading manufacturers tell me that, for the reasons I explained on a former occasion, these lulls are a necessity in that trade, and are likely to characterize it for scores of years to come. This is a most important peculiarity of a shoe town, as distinguished from the cotton town. *The floating population is the more floating on account of these lulls.* I have made no sweeping charges against the character of even this floating population. I said publicly, in the address which I gave two weeks ago, that I believed that if this population had homes, and was not floating, it would be as free from moral perils as any population of its size. We all know, and we all rejoice to know, that it *contains hundreds of most excellent people.* These very people, however, will be the last to accuse me of setting in too strong a light the perils of a floating population. Homelessness, I have said, is always a moral peril. And where, as here, a vast floating population congregates, the moral perils will always be found to be very great. He is pitiably ignorant of New England, and of this city, who does not know this. Now, it is out of this floating population, itself not sifted, that operatives are taken into the workrooms through a door that is itself not a sieve. And this is my second reason for asking for the separation of the sexes in the workrooms and the appointment of good moral men as overseers.

3. Thirty-three per cent of the operatives in your factories are changeable within the year, and you could not find out their characters if you would. In view of these circumstances it is very far from extrava-

gance to say that, in a city like this, the chances are extraordinarily great that bad men and bad women will occasionally be found in the work-rooms. This would be a probable theory antecedent to experience; but this city, and other cities having similar interests, exhibit an experience about which I should convince you that I know nothing, if I did not say that the experience justifies the theory.

4. *Foul mouths in factories are so well known that the expression is almost a proverb.* I make no unguarded charges. There are numerous and most honorable exceptions, especially in the factories managed on the clean system; but you would think me ill acquainted with the most essential parts of the subject I discuss, if I did not refer to what the best class of working men and working women speak of to me at every street corner. I need not expand this large consideration. It is a reason why the sexes should be separated in the workrooms. Unimportant as the circumstance may appear, it is not one of the least significant of the differences between a shoe factory and a cotton factory that in most of the rooms of the latter the machinery does, and in most of the rooms of the former does not, make noise enough to prevent conversation.

Utterly futile is it to compare, as I have heard a few white-handed critics carelessly do, the influences of the sexes on each other in these workrooms, filled at hap-hazard from a floating population through a door that is not a sieve, with their influences on each other in a high school. Woman's refining influence on man no one shall value more highly than I, but there is a proverb moderately well known among sensible men, to the effect that circumstances alter cases.* (1) In a high school the immoral are excluded. (2) The sexes mingled there have homes of their own, and are under the restraint of social ties close at hand. (3) They usually are persons who have refined tastes. (4) They are constantly under the eye of a teacher.

5. Physicians in this city, long resident here, calm, scholarly, well-balanced men, who have opportunity to see what a minister rarely sees, and what an employer sees as rarely, solemnly testify, after making careful allowance for every explanatory circumstance, that the influence of the mingling of the sexes in the workrooms of the vast trade of this city has been detrimental to the floating population in a very high degree. I must ask any one who does not see reasons for the separation of the sexes, and the appointment of good moral men as overseers, as two measures of importance in the factory system of the

*Note Cook's reference here to what was becoming known as the cult of true womanhood: the idea on the one hand that men tended to be bestial in character and women and marriage refined them, and on the other that men could corrupt women.

largest trade of the United States, to study this subject most carefully, as I have endeavored to do, from the point of view of judicious and candid local physicians.

6. Since the population is more largely floating, and the percentage of changeable operatives so much greater in a shoe town than in a cotton town, you cannot do as much with boarding-houses in a shoe town as in a cotton town. I think four or five boarding-houses here, under as good moral management as that of the best in the cotton towns, would be excellent capital, and ought to be erected; but any system of corporation boarding-houses, such as exists in the cotton towns, is almost an impossibility here, owing to the fact that you have five or seven thousand people who are here or not here, according as your vast business is at its brisk seasons or at its lulls.* *You cannot do as much with good boarding-houses in a shoe town as in a cotton town.* And therefore, since many of the moral measures that are commonly applied in manufacturing centres are inapplicable to shoe towns, those that can be applied become all the more important.

There are the wheels. Whoever does not keep fully in view these six points does not understand the complication of the problem of the moral condition of the shoe trade in a great city. My object here and now, as you notice, is only to keep before the public mind the important points of the topic, and to push personalities into the background. These are only very slight and inexhaustive hints of the reasons I have given, for the separation of the sexes in the workrooms and the appointment of good moral men as overseers. I solemnly believe that if all the factories of this city were managed as some five or six among the largest of them already are, on the system of the separation of the sexes and the appointment of good moral men as overseers in the workrooms, more good would result to the city than any ten churches here can do in a year. (Applause.) I beg you, my friends, not to applaud—if you can help it. And I believe that the factories here that do not attend to these points, but are more or less careless of the moral effect of the arrangements of their workrooms, do more to injure the moral condition of the city than any ten churches can do in a year to improve it. (Applause.) I stand for the right of the working men and women in the largest trade in the United States, now organizing a factory system of more importance than the cotton factory system, as it is to cover a larger public interest, to ask of their employers such workroom management

*The reference here is to the old monitored boardinghouses of Lowell and Lawrence. Ironically, by the 1870s most of the boardinghouses had switched to private hands and did not fit Cook's description.

as shall make the moral perils of the working class, and of their children, as few and small as possible. These perils will be great enough in any case. The working people have a right to ask that they be reduced to the smallest amount possible. This is the substance of all I have said; and I shall take back my words when Henry IV takes back his. (Applause.)

Two lies are in circulation that I must dispatch, and then the way will be open to the other theme I wish to introduce.

1. It is said that I have attacked the ministry of this city. It is wholly inaccurate to say that I have attacked the ministers. Whoever heard me two weeks ago to-night will remember that I quoted Tennyson's phrase about the "lily-handed, snow-banded, dilettante priest," but did not quote the last word, using "critic" instead of it; and I had in mind no minister. I said the theme was complicated, and that every minister must direct his own course of study. I would not have dared to speak on it myself without three months attention to it. It may very well be that, in the midst of multiplied activities, this or that public speaker, heartily interested in this theme, does not take it up because it cannot well be touched without a large attention to it. Speakers must choose their topics according to the course of their previous studies. The adaptations of men to this or that line of effort differ; and nothing is more juvenile or mischievous than that good men, taking different lines of effort according to their different adaptations, should therefore seem to themselves or to the public not to agree. All my relations with the ministry of this city are, and always have been, cordial in the extreme. I must say that I have myself seen service in battle at other points of the line of the enemy, and therefore sympathize with those leading the attack at those points, and have no fear that I shall be understood as underrating the importance of attack at any other point on account of attacking at this. I confess I think the moral condition of this city a legitimate subject for its pulpit; and the moral condition of the factories is a highly important part of that theme, and not the less important for being endlessly delicate and complicated. Those who labor in respect to this matter indirectly will not blame me for attacking it directly. The theme is not only complicated, but new; and, as the years pass, the responsibilities of the pulpit in regard to it will increase.*

2. In regard to a matter which has been persistently used to turn against me the working men, I have nothing to say, except that it has been used in vain. It is in no sense other than that of a reiteration or

*Here Cook foreshadows the emergence of the social gospel movement.

more specific statement of what I have said or implied before, that I allude to the matter now, in order to make the air wholly clear for the theme which I wish to introduce.

(1) Before my lecture of January 22d, I said repeatedly in private that I had no charges to make against the *present* character of a certain room, the place of which has been so unnecessarily mentioned in the public prints. Several gentlemen remember that they heard me say then, and I say now, that I think the *present* character of the room very good.

(2) I saw but six girls in the room, and one of these was pointed out to me as an exception to the rest. I vividly remember that one was pointed out as an exception. One of the six, I am told on excellent authority, has left the room since. To only four, therefore, of the eight whom I have been charged with accusing, would any remark of my own apply.

INTRODUCTION TO LECTURE 4

The controversies stirred up in the city by Cook continued to generate capacity crowds for his lectures, as well as a counter–lecture series. By Lecture IV Cook had become an important and controversial figure, and his lecture series had become a major source of entertainment for the city. At the end of Lecture III a listener had raised such vehement objection to Cook's comments that he was forcibly removed from the hall and arrested by the police, and the demand to hear Cook's fourth lecture was so great that even before the doors opened a capacity crowd had gathered at the doors. Within a few minutes after admittance was allowed every seat in the hall was filled. Since Lecture IV was not given to the papers to reprint, and it is not available in any complete form, what follows is a transcription which appeared in the local paper rather than the actual text.

In Lecture IV Cook put forth his solution to the increased conflict of the new industrial society. Having already documented the increase in social discord and the decline of the policing power of the traditional family, Cook now pointed to the church and schools as the new police for moral order. In his view, these institutions transcended class divisions and could bring together society in a hierarchical moral structure. In this new moral order Cook saw cooperation between labor and capital, but not the cooperative society envisioned by the Knights of St. Crispin.

4. SOCIAL CONTROL: THE CHURCH AND THE SCHOOL

Mr. Cook began by an allusion to Clark's Island, almost within view, in Massachusetts Bay, where the exploring expedition sent from the

Mayflower rested, in spite of the necessity for labor and haste, on the Sabbath before the landing of the Pilgrims. Robert C. Winthrop, in his oration at Plymouth, at the recent two hundred and fiftieth anniversary of the landing, said that the Sabbath is of such importance that the most appropriate place for a monument to the Pilgrims is Clark's Island.

1. The same difficulties between Labor and Capital which have arisen in Old England will arise in New England, as soon as our population is thick enough.

2. On account of the social and political position of the American working men, as compared with that of the European, Capital here, in adjusting its relations to Labor, cannot take the high and mighty method on the one hand, or the patronizing method on the other, both of which are so common in Europe.

3. It follows that, although the problem concerning the relations of Capital and Labor is the same in the New World as in the Old World, it must of necessity be treated in the New World, not in the Old World way, but in a New World way. The American industrial difficulties must have a peculiarly American treatment.

4. It will be found that the only bridge which will carry a free Civilization safely over Barbarism and let its feet through at no point, is the Bible laid on the buttresses of the Sundays. The chasm between Capital and Labor can never be bridged in the United States, as it has been in England, by a kid glove. It can never be bridged in the United States, as it has been on the continent of Europe, by a bayonet. It can be bridged only by the Bible laid on the buttresses of the Sundays and the Common Schools. The nature of republican institutions is such that the chasm between Capital and Labor can be effectually bridged in the United States only by love, and not by force; only by intelligence and integrity in the opposing forces, and not by aristocratic prestige; that is, only by the Bible laid on the buttresses of the Sundays and of the Common Schools; and on neither the one nor the other of these two sets of buttresses taken by itself, though on the former alone much better than on the latter alone.

There exist, therefore, two sets of reasons why working men should make a right use of Sunday—the Industrial and the Religious.

I. *The Industrial Reasons.*

1. The right use of Sunday by working men, or public worship held by all classes as equals in one assembly, has an important tendency to diminish distance of feeling between rich and poor.

2. The right use of Sunday by working men has an important tendency to interest the largest, a well-educated, the most widely-heard,

and the most conscientious class of public speakers, in the study of the wants of working men.

3. The right use of Sunday by working men has an important tendency to interest the largest, a well-educated, the most widely-heard, and the most conscientious class of public speakers, in the public discussion of the wants of working men.

4. On account of these three circumstances, the right use of Sunday by working men has an important tendency to make the church, which holds both rich and poor, such a means of allaying prejudice and securing mutual understanding, justice, and good-will, as to give it much the same relations to the different classes in society at large, as the Industrial Board of Arbitration or Conference has in particular cases of conflict.

5. Cheap Homes, Hours of Labor, Wages, Factory Reform, Temperance, all causes of the utmost importance to the industrial interests of working men, have among the masses of the members of the churches a vast amount of unexpressed sympathy, now largely wasted, and which a right use of the Sabbath by working men might do much, directly and indirectly, to turn into channels of the very highest value to those industrial interests.

6. The great principle of Co-operation, which is the hope of the cause of Labor, depends peculiarly for its success upon a high degree of self-control, integrity, and mutual confidence in moral character, between those who co-operate. This self-control and moral confidence have been proved, by the experience of associative effort in Europe and the United States, to be the cement without which the stones in the temple of Co-operation most assuredly cannot be laid; and the Sundays are the trowels for the making and the laying of that cement.

7. It is the great interest of working men to preserve Sunday as a day of rest; but to neglect it as a day of worship is to undermine its authority as a day of rest.

These dead, backward, mossy churches are said by some to have no sympathy with working men. But they put Sunday on the statute-book, and keep it there, the only day of rest working men have. Undermine Sabbath as a day of worship, make it only a legal holiday, and it cannot be preserved as a day of rest.

II.*The Religious Reasons.*

1. Sunday is God's day; the Sermon on the Mount re-institutes the moral spirit of the whole Decalogue; not one jot or tittle of the law, that is, of the Decalogue, is to fail; and, although Christianity transferred the Sabbath from the seventh to the first day of the week, the moral

spirit of the fourth commandment is as fully reinstituted by the Sermon on the Mount as that of the seventh or eighth.

2. It is becoming more and more a proposition of science and scepticism itself, that the education of the moral and religious nature is the very highest of the interests of the individual man and of society at large. But this education is not furnished by schools, or adequately by literature. The best school civilization now presents for the education of what is highest in man is the right use of the church and of Sundays.

3. Children of parents who neglect the Sabbath are likely as a mass to go further than their parents in such neglect, falling behind, in moral and religious character, other children who have the benefit of the admirably equipped Sabbath Schools and of the whole right use of Sunday.

4. In a great city, the Sabbath is the worst day of dissipation.

5. Indispensable as legal aids to religion are, religion can never be enacted by law; the doors of the dram-shop, the gambling-house, and, indeed, of the poor-house, cannot be shut by reforms as to wages and hours of labor merely. The self-control induced by moral and religious education must supplement the effect of these reforms, or those doors cannot be shut.

6. An important moral and religious influence is exerted upon a population by its simply meeting once a week *in clean clothes and in sacred places and for public devotion,* whatever may be said of the poorness of sermons, although the average of sermons is as good as the average of Congressional speeches.

7. Sunday kept holy is a delight. Poor clothes, rear pews and hard work do not keep the Catholic working men from attending church. Is it possible that American working men are more influenced by a necessity existing in these excuses than the Catholic?* It is not enough to say that the Catholic church has free seats. There are other churches with free seats; but they are not full. It is not enough to say that a peculiar influence is exerted by priest over people. There are churches where personal affection between speaker and hearer amounts to an influence of a similar kind; but these are not full. If hard work is the excuse for not attending church, the ten thousand in this city who habitually neglect the Sabbath ought to fill the churches in the lulls of the trade of the city, which twice a year throw hundreds of workmen

---

*Note that Cook juxtaposes American workingmen with Catholic workingmen. Although Cook is not directly attacking the Catholic Church by comparing Catholic workers with American workers, he is reinforcing the idea that Catholics are lower status, i.e., not Americans.

out of work. But the churches then are not full. Individual cases of hardship may exist in which these excuses have real force; but beneath the weight of the reasons that have been given for the right use of Sunday, they crack as an eggshell.

—*Lynn Semi Weekly Reporter*, March 14, 1871.

INTRODUCTION TO LECTURE 5

Once again the city of Lynn filled the Music Hall to capacity; several dozen people were left standing, and the volunteer choir was forced to sit on the stage. Cook, playing upon the excitement generated by his earlier lectures, depicted himself as an embattled reformer attacked unjustly by the immoral manufacturers. Before beginning his formal talk, he mentioned that from the accusations of his opponents one would assume that he was "the most unpopular man in this city." But he claimed his cause to be just, and it was that justice, he declared, which led to his "being obliged to repress applause here night after night." Cook's confidence and sense of his own importance grew as he continued to meet with supportive audiences. He became increasingly convinced of his role as a savior of industrial society. In this lecture Cook continued with his comparison of shoe towns and textile towns. He then moved beyond the present to the future, claiming that if the present were not reformed the future would deteriorate into moral decay. In that battle to save the future our good Reverend Mr. Cook became the major embattled hero, throwing his "whole weight into the scale against the continuance of these careless arrangements."

5. SHOE TOWN (LYNN) COMPARED TO TEXTILE TOWNS (LOWELL AND LAWRENCE)

One of the pastors of the city volunteered to me the opinion that his church endorses me as fully as my own, in its official and public resolution. It is not unimportant to notice that the Catholic pulpit of Lynn has put itself in print fully on the side of the two measures which have been suggested, although, on account of inaccurate information as to what I said publicly, denouncing me for injuring the reputation of the city. In view of the extraordinary misrepresentations which have abounded, this tone of public sentiment has the higher significance. Persistent efforts have been made to turn the city against me. But the city persistently refuses to be turned. Six weeks have now passed. There has been time for public sentiment to become calm and intelligent.

I am honestly proud of this city for its present attitude. From Boston to Chicago, Lynn has been praised in the religious papers, and in some of the secular, for that attitude. I must solemnly beg leave to inform the group of capitalists and manufacturers and the inextensive circle of the dependents, who constitute the only offended parties here, that there are twenty-seven thousand persons in Lynn who are not capitalists or manufacturers. To-day Lynn stands as a queen, clothed in the prosperity of her last twenty years, her schools and churches and libraries glittering among her jewels, and she puts one hand on the great factories here that are careful of the moral effect of their arrangements, and says: Give me more of these; and she puts the finger of the other hand in scorn upon the factories that are careless of the moral effect of their arrangements, and says: Give me fewer of these!

Wide Contrasts Between a Shoe Town and a Cotton Town

Six circumstances of great importance distinguish a shoe town, like Lynn, from a cotton town, like Lawrence or Lowell. The shoe trade has, and the cotton trade has not, two periods of comparative inactivity each year, and thousand of operatives in those periods are thrown out of work. The best kind of shoes, and especially ladies' shoes, to the production of which this city devotes the largest part of its industry, change their fashions with the seasons. Cotton does not change its fashions. You may safely accumulate cotton cloth. But it will not do to accumulate a stock of outgrown fashions in shoes. The new fashions cannot be foreseen for months in advance. And besides this, the new machinery invented for the processes of the shoe trade makes production so rapid that many manufacturers assign overproduction as the chief cause of the lulls. At any rate, when the market is full, buyers have sellers at their mercy. The law of the trade is not to accumulate shoes, but to fill orders for shoes. At certain periods of the year, orders for shoes pour in and a brisk period of work ensues. The orders grow fewer, and a lull ensues. The orders pour in again when the new fashions have been determined, and brisk work follows once more. The orders wane and work wanes. For all these reasons it is to be expected that, while production continues as rapid as it now is, and by the invention of new machinery it is growing more rapid every day, lulls will characterize the shoe trade fully enough to distinguish that trade broadly from the coal, the iron, or the cotton, which produce articles in the very nature of which there does not inhere, as there does inhere in the very nature of the article produced by the shoe trade, a constant susceptibility to change of fashion. Various expedients can, and I hope will, be used to shorten these lulls; but all of the many manufacturers with whom I have conversed consider lulls an outgrowth of necessity in the structure of the trade, and working men know well that to counteract their effect is one of the problems of their industrial life.

Everything cannot be done in a shoe town that can be done in a cotton town; but there is more need for something to be done; and, therefore, what can be done is the more important; and what can be done is to separate the sexes in the workrooms, and to take the utmost care in the appointment of moral men as overseers. The most of the rooms of a shoe factory differ from the most of those in a cotton factory, in that in the former the machinery does not, and in the latter does, make noise enough to prevent free conversation between operatives; and, unimportant as this difference may appear, it is in itself, and especially in connection with the four circumstances already mentioned, by no means one of the least significant of the wide contrasts in the problems to which the cotton factory system and the shoe factory system are to be adjusted. In the cotton towns the greatest pains have been taken with the excellent corporation boarding-houses. Each boarding-house of this class accommodates either men or women exclusively. But I see no reason why the sexes should be separated in the workrooms under the control of the cotton factory system. The large factories here are individual enterprises, and not the property of corporations as in Lawrence or Lowell. The consequence is that if the leader of the business in any factory is disposed to be careful as to his arrangements, he can have his own way easily, for he has only himself to consult; and if he is disposed to be careless he can have his own way, for the same reason; and in the latter case can have it more easily than if in a corporation, competing, as every great corporation at Lawrence or Lowell does, with some other great corporation, and this in regard to the moral as well as the material welfare of the operative population.

Exigencies Likely to Arise in the Future of Manufacturing Centres in New England

So much on the contrast between a shoe town and a cotton town. Already this city has a population of five or seven thousand who are here or not according as business is at its brisk period or at its lulls. How large will that population be in ten years? How large in twenty? I am in Lynn but for a moment; but I profess to care enough for it to keep fifty and a hundred years of its future in view, and to put at hazard any popularity I may or might have in this city, by asking you to meet, as men, the complicated problems of your vast industry, and not set a careless precedent for that crowded future. If the population of this city increases for the next twenty years as it has for the last twenty, you will have, before the end of that time, or soon thereafter, a floating population of ten or fifteen thousand.

Now, is there a man—*who* is the man and *where* is the man—who will say that you can have a tide of ten or fifteen thousand people swirling in and out of a city like this and no moral perils arise, no sediment be stirred, no grave responsibilities laid upon those whose business is the floodgate through which these tides must mingle with the other tides of the population?

At the best, the filter that you can provide for the tides will be ineffective enough; but to say that there is need of no filter, that you may safely take the chances of the present factory arrangements being continued here, is to say—what time will disprove. If the present careless factory arrangements are continued fifty years, you will have a city full of moral ulcers. Lazarus will lie at the gate of Dives in this city, and he will be full of sores. I throw my whole weight into the scale against the continuance of these careless arrangements. *I know that the American Lazarus may to-morrow, or in the next generation, become a Dives, as the European may not; but, in spite of American institutions, the day is coming, unless factory life is studied and adjusted most carefully, when here and through-out New England, of which the whole Atlantic slope is a factory, Lazarus will lie at the gate of Dives.*

INTRODUCTION TO LECTURE 6

In Lecture 6 Cook links together his concern for the growth of the factory system with the growth of cities themselves.

Although America had been increasingly urbanized since the turn of the nineteenth century, it was the post-Civil-War period in which this urbanization process made its greatest impact on the American mind. Cities such as Boston, New York, Philadelphia, Baltimore in the East, and Pittsburgh, Chicago, and St. Louis in the West attracted thousands of immigrants and reached proportions unimagined in the antebellum period. The institutions that had given shape and substance to prewar America seemed to decline as the urban centers grew. The churches in these new urban communities seemed to lose significance for the citizens of the new city. The increase in the size and influence of the larger cities gave rise to a fear among those familiar with small town and rural America that they were losing their influence as well. Joseph Cook, who came out of rural America but did not reject the potential of the new urban environment, looked to the church for control and influence over the new urban masses. His solution to the problems of the growing urban centers, like his solutions to the growing divisions between rich and poor, was for the church to take the lead in moral reform and by moral reform to bring the new urban masses into harmony with a society controlled and dominated by others.

Cook's concern for the distance between the churchgoers and the urban masses, like his concern for the growing division between rich and poor, reflects the unifying element in the social gospel movement. Ultimately, this movement comes to fruition in the early twentieth century, with the publication of Walter Rauchen-busch's Christianity and the Social Crisis[71] *in 1907, and the Reverend Joseph Cook himself comes to be the major spokesperson for the conservative wing of that movement. At this stage, however, Cook is just beginning to raise the questions that ultimately come to dominate the thinking of the leading urban Protestant ministers by the end of the century.*

As in his previous lectures, Cook filled the hall to standing room only. Talking from notes, Cook did not have a finished lecture to give to the local papers. This lecture, like Lecture 4, is only a newspaper synopsis and lacks Cook's normal style.

6. INDUSTRIALIZATION AND URBANIZATION

1. It is a remarkable fact that the growth of the average population of the cities of the United States between 1850 and 1860 was more than twice as great as that of the population of the whole country. In the census of 1860 a list of one hundred and twenty-six cities is given, scattered through the whole territory of the Union, and the average increase of their population between 1850 and 1860 was 78.62 per cent, while that of the whole population of the United States during the same period was only 35.59 per cent. In this period, the increase of the population of New York was 56 per cent; of Philadelphia, 60; of Worcester, 46; of Hartford, 115; of New Haven, 93; of Buffalo, 91; of Nashville, 62; of New Orleans, 44; of St. Louis, 106; of Chicago, 264.

2. The growth of the population of the cities of Europe is much more rapid than that of the whole of any single nation of Europe. From 1832 to 1869 the increase of the population of London was 98 percent; of Constantinople, 50; of Paris, 118; of Vienna, 107; of Moscow, 50; of Berlin, 220; of Manchester, 49; of Liverpool, 174; of Madrid, 105. Liverpool has increased as rapidly as Boston, Berlin more rapidly than New York.

3. It is evident from the two preceding propositions that there is at present a tendency of population, here and abroad, to mass itself in cities; and, it will be found on examination, that this tendency has been exhibiting itself in greater and greater force for the last fifty years.

4. The growth of means of intercommunication has been a chief feature of the last fifty years. The Atlantic Cables, the Pacific Railway, the Suez Canal, with the infinite multiplication of subsidiary railways and telegraphs, are introducing a new set of circumstances into civilization.

5. It will be found that the growth and influence of great cities increase with every increase of the means of intercommunication between States; but the increase of such means of intercommunication, as has just been shown, is very nearly the most characteristic feature of the present age. The current of population is governed by the law of supply and demand. The demand is for population at centres, since these furnish opportunities to industry and capital not found elsewhere. But the creation of such centres, easily intercommunicating, is a permanent result of the growth of the means of intercommunication.

6. The problem of the perishing classes in our cities increases in importance with every increase of this tendency of population to mass itself in centres. Every addition to the growth and influence of great cities adds importance and amplification to that problem.

7. Frontier life is essentially a struggle for food, shelter, and raiment. We honor that life on the slopes of the Rocky Mountains. It has an historical glory in the story of the first winter of the Pilgrims at Plymouth, where Rose Standish and half of those who came over in the *Mayflower* laid down in the graves on the slope of the hill across the Bay yonder, in a struggle simply for food, shelter, and raiment. But this same struggle is carried on in our cities. There is a frontier life in cities. It is the fiercest of all forms of the struggle for food, shelter, and raiment. More than half the companies that enter this struggle perish, and many a Rose Standish among them. As the struggle is fiercer than ordinary frontier life, it deserves proportionate honor. A light thing to meet the wolves of ordinary frontier life, or any beasts of the forest, compared with meeting the wolves of city frontier life, the dram-shop, the gambling-saloon, the places nearer the pit than either of these, the high rents, the competitions. To keep the wolf from the door is a thing that means more in city frontier life than in ordinary frontier life.

8. It follows from all the preceding propositions that the churches of great cities are now more than ever called to consider the condition of the poor in great cities. If Providence were to write its will on the sky, it

would not declare more clearly than it now does, by the leading events of the century, the duty of the church to study the problem of the perishing classes in the great centres of population.

Whoever has not pity enough for the poor to see this duty of the church written in the great and imposing events of Providence in this century, or to regard the occasional discussion, in the churches of our crowded centres of population, of the responsibilities of all other classes toward the poor, as the gospel, either does not know the gospel, or is not a man, but a wolf! (Applause.) What the speaker was about to say would be only the expansion and *application* of the sublime passages of the Scripture just read before the audience.

Mr. Cook then proceeded to consider:

I. *Cheap Homes.* To illustrate the connections of the moral with the daily physical and social conditions of a population in its homes, Mr. Cook drew a picture of a tenement-house he had visited in Boston, so crowded and dilapidated and unclean that the observance of the common decencies of life was an impossibility in it.

1. The physical health of the poor is their capital in trade; but narrow, crowded, illy-lighted, poorly-warmed, and filthy tenement-houses exert an influence on the physical health so damaging and deadly that the industrial force of a population may be diminished one-half simply by putting the population into such houses.*

2. The moral health of the poor is the least withered, and almost the only, source of their happiness: the hearthstone is usually more to a poor man than to a rich man, for it is all a poor man has: moral health in the family is the only fire that can warm the hearthstone; and the most pestilent and deadly of the effects of crowded and neglected tenement-houses is the undermining of the moral health of the occupants.

3. Tenement-houses so crowded and dilapidated and unclean that the observance of the common decencies of life is an impossibility in them, are schools of vice for the children that must be brought up in them.

4. Houses of this class are nestling-places for the city wolves. Intemperance and other of the fierce beasts of the city forest roam abroad through the population in houses of this class, as if through natural and indefeasible hunting ranges; and find there fat prey (not the fattest, for the richer class oftener furnishes that, but the most accessible and indefensible, because of the disheartening influence of poverty when the moral heat has gone out of the hearthstone).

*Good conditions for the poor permit good healthy workers for industry. Thus charity is also good business.

5. A double price is usually paid by the poor, who are so crowded that they must buy by the parcel and cannot buy by the mass. The poor in crowded tenement-houses in our cities are forced to buy coal by the basket and not by the ton, and wood by the bundle and not by the mass, not only because they have not money to buy more, but because they have no place to store more; and whoever is obliged to buy by the basket or bundle and not by the mass, pays, on the average, a double price.

6. *Unless two conditions can be secured, cheap rents in situations near a city, and cheap railway fares, to and from those situations, the poorest in a city cannot go out of the city to obtain lodgings.*

7. Effort has been successfully made of late in many of the cities of Germany to secure the first of these conditions. The co-operative savings banks of Germany have been managed on such a plan that large amounts of capital have been put at the disposal of companies of working men for the establishment of cheap homes in the immediate vicinity of great cities.

8. Effort is now being made on a quite large scale in Boston to secure not only the first of these conditions, but the first and second in combination. To combine the two is a peculiarly American idea, which Mr. Josiah Quincy has the high honor of adding to the German plan and bringing before the Massachusetts Legislature.

9. After the repairs are paid for on property rented to the poor, the rent should not be much higher than the legal rate of interest on the amount of capital invested. John Ruskin managed a mass of tenement-houses in London in this plan as an example to England against usurious rents; and found the occupants, who had paid rents of twenty and thirty per cent, and of whom he required only five percent, soon able to buy of him a twelve years lease.

10. So far as the solution of the problem of the perishing classes in cities can be promoted by cheap homes, low rents and cheap railway fares, it is evident that the sooner a city gives its attention to the problem the better.

11. This city is growing so rapidly that it may be said that the sun has not risen here on any morning for a year without shining on some new roof. As many buildings have been erected or remodelled here during the last year as there are days in the year. Since 1850 the population has increased one hundred per cent. Since 1865 it has increased thirty-six per cent. The city has yet a village-like character in the connection of plats of land with the great mass of its dwelling-houses. *It is endlessly important that this character be, as far as possible, preserved; and that pestilent tenement-houses be kept out from the first by following the best models in the construction of lodging-houses, but especially by doing everything to promote the*

establishment of cheap homes. Mr. Cook commended this subject to the serious attention of the Board of Trade.*

II. *Boarding-houses.* In discussing this part of the topic, Mr. Cook made two preliminary remarks:

1. This city cannot imitate the corporation boarding-houses of Lawrence and Lowell, for there are no corporations here, and the manufacturing population is more largely floating than it is in the cities named.

2. A careful attention to the subject of boarding-houses is seen at Lawrence and Lowell; and that careful attention may be imitated, and ought to be imitated, in this city, until a plan has been found adapted to the peculiar circumstances of Lynn.

Mr. Cook then proceeded to quote ten points from printed regulations in force in the corporation boarding-houses of Lawrence:

1. "No tenement will be leased to persons of immoral or intemperate habits; and any tenant who, after occupancy, shall be found of such habits, or to receive boarders of such habits, will be notified to vacate the premises."

2. "A suitable chamber for the sick must be reserved in each boarding-house, so that they may not be annoyed by others occupying the same room."

3. "Males and females must not board in the same house, without special permission from the agent."

4. "The doors of the boarding-houses will be closed at ten o'clock, P.M., and no one admitted after that time, unless some reasonable excuse can be given."

5. "Nor must company be had at unreasonable hours, and in no case after twelve o'clock at night."

6. "If any boarders are rude or disorderly, or attend improper or disreputable places of amusement, their names must be reported at the counting-room, and they will be discharged."

7. "A proper observance of the Sabbath being equally essential to the formation of good habits and good morals, the preservation of good character, as well as the maintenance of good order, all persons in the employ of this company are expected and required to have some regular place of public worship in town, and to be as uniform in attendance thereat as possible. In every church in town seats will [be] furnished gratuitously, if desired, on application on the Sabbath to the sexton of the parish; and such seats may be regularly occupied, till notice is given to the contrary."

---

*See Sam Bass Warner, *Street Car Suburbs* (Cambridge: Atheneum, 1962) for a discussion of how this process occurred in Boston from 1870 to 1900.

8. "On no account must company be received at the boarding-houses during the hours of public worship, nor at any time on the Sabbath will rudeness, disorder, or games of any sort be permitted. Persons holding subordinate positions in these mills, who neglect this regulation, need not expect promotion when vacancies occur."

9. "The above regulations are considered as a part of the contract with each person entering the employment of the _____ Cotton Mills, and the Company will require a strict compliance therewith."

10. "I hereby assent to the regulations within, a copy of which I have duly received," is the form of printed words endorsed as a part of the contract, with blanks for name, room, date, and a witness of the signature.

It is exceedingly significant that, after an experience of fifty years, these regulations as to boarding-houses have been found *necessary* in the cotton towns, where one of the most usual forms of the contract with operatives, as appears from the published rules of the mills at Lawrence and Lowell, is, that the contract holds for one year. Contracts with operatives in the shoe towns are so far from being made on this plan, that thirty-three per cent of the operatives here are changeable within the year. It can hardly be supposed, therefore, that if the regulations just quoted are needed in the cotton towns, any *less* careful ones are *needed* in the shoe towns, the floating population is likely to be so much larger in the latter; although it is this very circumstance, and the fact that the shoe factories are individual enterprises and not corporations, which prevents any system of corporation boarding-houses from arising in the latter. It is very important to notice what the *usual* definition of a respectable boarding-house is. Daniel Webster, in a legal case where an agent had lost a large sum of money by not depositing it in a safe, told the jury that the man did not take the *usual* method of keeping the money safely, and over and over repeated with emphasis that the *usual* method had not been taken, until the jury were saturated with a conviction that not to take the *usual* method in such a case was carelessness, justifying the legal action brought against the agent. The *usual* method in respectable boarding-houses, where both gentlemen and ladies are received, is to have two sections of the house, more or less defined, assigned to each class, and not to sandwich rooms of all sorts together, or to lease a vacant room to any one as soon as vacated, especially not to any stranger. When the *usual* method of respectable boarding-houses is followed, Mr. Cook had no objection to boarding-houses where both sexes are received; but it was notorious in this city that the women were often obliged to take the poorest rooms at the boarding-houses. There ought to be two drawing-rooms in each boarding-house of any considerable size—one for gentlemen and one for ladies,—a bath-room, and a room that could be given at any time to the sick.

Mr. Cook then proceeded to offer six reasons why the Woman's Union for Christian Work, one of the established charities of the city, should have funds placed at its disposal for the erection of a boarding-house.

1. The Woman's Union assert, in their last published Report, that "multitudes" of women, "mostly young, who come from distant homes to engage for a few months in the year in some branch" of the vast trade of this city, are "unable to obtain here comfortable, or even respectable, boarding-places." (Report of 1870, p. 12.)

2. They further assert that, on account of the reason just given, "multitudes" of women, "mostly young," "separated from home influences and home joys, are almost driven, from the nature of things, to seek diversion in the streets, or at undesirable places of public amusement" (p. 12).

3. They inform the public that they have "long aimed to have under their control a well-conducted boarding-house for young women" (p. 13). This enterprise is likely to fail for want of funds. It is a shame—it is a shame which it will require no little benevolence and activity to erase, that, in a city where three or four thousand depend on boarding-houses, the enterprise of this noble charity to open a boarding-house that might be a model, for others in the city, should fail for the want of five thousand dollars, or of ten. (Applause.)

4. The Woman's Union is a charity under management that can be trusted. Its committees are the wives of the capitalists and manufacturers of the city.

5. The Woman's Union is confident that, if the enterprise could once be started, it would be a financial success, and support itself.

6. The success of one excellently conducted boarding-house under the control of this established charity, Mr. Cook thought, might be a means of suggesting the right solution of one of the most complicated problems connected with the floating population of shoe towns, namely, how boarding-houses can be what they should be, when a system of corporation boarding-houses is impossible. Try one boarding-house under the control of this charity. If it succeeds financially, rich men here, separately or in company, ought to establish a second and appoint its regulations; and, if that should succeed, a third, until the supply should be found equal to the demand. Mr. Cook said he had volunteered his remarks for the Woman's Union, and was interested in their enterprise, not only for its own sake, but as a means of threading a

needle for the future of Lynn, and of cities having similar problems to solve.*—*Lynn Semi-Weekly Reporter*, March 22, 1871.

INTRODUCTION TO LECTURE 7

With the coming of spring weather Cook moved from the topic of the potential corruption of the factory system to the more titillating topic of personal vice. As John Harvey Kellogg (who helped found the cereal company) and the Women's Christian Temperance Union would do later, Cook frightened his audience with references to vice-induced physical degeneration. Like other moral reformers of the period, he began by extolling the virtues of higher bliss against sensual pleasure. He buttressed this argument by claiming that medical science would prove the degeneracy of baser pleasures. In this argument Cook linked together science and the Scriptures to distinguish between the artificial passions of pleasure and the natural passions of higher bliss. Making sure not to leave any areas of possible support untapped, Cook used a body politic metaphor and cited the Unionist position against secession to emphasize his point.

Having alerted his audiences to the signs of vice, Cook then linked "moral purity" to the quasi-scientific idea of the supposed "racial purity" and superiority of the Anglo-Saxons. Picking up on the work of the disaffected French racialist Arthur Gobineau, whose work (first translated into English in 1856) had a major impact in both America and Germany, Cook argued that the Anglo-Saxon race, which "rules the world today," drew its strength from its origins in the German forests. "The hiding of the power of the Anglo-Saxon race has been in the fact that it was at the first free from the sin of Sodom and Gomorrah. That race is passing the trial of luxury." Cook embraced the idea of the racial superiority of the Anglo-Saxons, but claimed that the nature of that superiority rested in their moral purity. To lose moral purity would also mean a loss of racial superiority.

Cook's tales of purity and vice, like his attack on the corrupting influence of the factory system, kept the Music Hall filled to capacity despite "weather most attractive . . . for promenading," and the competing lecture of an "Escaped Nun" attacking the evils of the Catholic Church.

7. PURITY AND VICE

1. The power of high and rich and pure affection *in all its forms* is the first remedy for bad habits. Blessed is love; for it is the antagonist of every form of coarse passion. The duty of giving free scope to pure and high friendships, to all the affections of home, and to every worthy and

---

*This idea was later picked up by Jacob Riis with his proposal, "Philanthrophy's 5%" See Riis, *How the Other Half Lives*

rich affection, and all this as a remedy for bad habits, was here inculcated in strong terms.

2. *The superiority of bliss to pleasure* may now be considered in established doctrine in the fixed portions of the knowledge science possesses of human nature. By bliss, is to be understood the delight of all the rich and high and pure affections; by pleasure, what the world calls such. Three points are pushed into great prominence even by infidelity in the most recent theories of human nature: (1) All bliss in the faculties arises from their activity; (2) The moral faculties have a natural supremacy in the mind; (3) The higher any faculty, the greater the bliss of its exercise. It is one of the commonest, and one of the most significant assertions of physicians, that the pleasures of the vices are a thousandfold overrated by the young, by imagination previous to experience. This is true of intemperance. It is true throughout the whole range of the vices, mental as well as physical. It is a circumstance of the deepest significance that the infamous portions of the populations of great cities like London, Berlin, and New York, are commonly estimated by the authors who have written the most elaborately on this subject, to be changed once in about seven years, one-half by death under the diseases which are the great red seal of the Lord Almighty's wrath, but one-half by *disgust.*

3. The third remedy suggested was *a distinction between the artificial and the natural passions.* Mr. Cook drew attention to this distinction as a point of great importance in recent science and illustrating scores of pasages of the Scriptures. How are we to know what appetite is natural, and what artificial? Is there a test which is itself not artificial, but which any honest man may apply? *A natural appetite,* Mr. Cook held, *does not increase its forces on gratification; while every artificial appetite does increase its force on gratification. The two are to be distinguished by this broad difference.* In the appetite for food, gratification of the natural appetite, induced by the vice of gluttony, by high living, or by dyspeptic disease, the gratification of the appetite only increases its force. The same is true of thirst that is true of hunger. The distinction between the natural and the artificial state of the former appetite is of endless importance in explaining the sorceries of intemperance. The gratification of thirst in its natural state, and this for a lifetime, does not increase its force. The gratification of it in its artificial state, and this for only a year, a month, or, in some cases, for only a day, so increases its forces that this appetite alone is found fully competent to ruin both body and soul. This distinction between the natural and the artificial appetites is to be applied through the whole range of human nature.

4. *Abstinence from any physical and seated habit, in order to be successful, must be total and this not only in act, but in imagination.* This is the organizing principle of the best recent systems of remedial treatment for the intemperate. Dr. Day, formerly of the Binghampton Inebriate Asylum, and now of Massachusetts makes a rigid adherence to this medical precept the first object to be secured in the case of every patient. Dr. Mandsley's recent investigations as to the effect of alcohol upon the brain show that the microscopic cells of that structure are changed in size, shape, and color by the habit of intemperance; that these changes endure after the habit has been broken off; and that there are physical reasons in the changes why one who has had a seated habit of intemperance cannot reform, except by an abstinence that is total. Dr. Day states that he witnessed the dissection of the brain of a person for many years in practice of total abstinence, but once an inebriate, and found the microscopic cells still in the weak and unnatural state produced by the earlier indulgences. Thousands of the intemperate, who make the most heroic effort to escape their bondage, fail to do so because they do not begin far enough back. It is the doctrine of recent science that there are physical reasons why abstinence, to be successful, must be total; and that it is necessary to resist, not merely the first glass, but the first *thought* of the first glass; that is, to lay the check where the Scriptures long ago laid it, namely, on the *imagination.* This principle applies to every seated vice. It is found to be the only spear of Ithuriel of temper celestial enough to touch "The toad squat at the ear of Eve," and make the fiend within start up in his true shape.

5. *No one part of the soul is to be allowed to act without the unforced consent of every other part.* It is a portion of the fundamental law of the United States that no one State is to declare war, or make peace, without the consent of every other State. This is also a fundamental law of the republic of the human faculties; and by it is determined what is, and what is not, *natural* action for any one of these faculties. The base of the brain is not to be allowed to act without the consent of the top of the brain. It cannot be that man is so skilfully made that the natural action of his faculties is discord. But the very nature of vice is, that it introduce South Carolinas into the republic of the soul and these declare war or make peace without the consent of all the other States. No vice can carry a unanimous vote of all the faculties. Any action of the soul that does not carry a unanimous vote of the faculties is unnatural. The soul is made on a plan, as much as the eye, the ear, or the hand. *The soul acts naturally only when its action produces continuous joy in all the faculties. No joy is natural that is not full.* The adoption of the principle that no basilar

faculty is to be allowed to act without the consent of the coronal faculties, would uproot vice in any soul. Let there be no South Carolinas among the faculties, and there can be no civil war.

6. It is of incalculable worth as a remedy for bad habits, to fasten on the mind, what the advances of recent sciences so startlingly demonstrate, that *no habitual vice can be permanently concealed.* In discussing what recent science teaches as to the signs of the vices, endless care is to be taken on two points:

(1) A suspicious temper is to be thrust aside; for, at the best, mistakes in reading character will be made. Perhaps a percentage of ten in a hundred judgments will be mistakes at the very best. Signs of the vices, and of diseases or of hereditary taints, must not be confounded. The pasteboard complexion of the student, and the lustreless complexion induced by certain physical vices must not be confused with each other. The flurry of nerves unstrung by hard work must be distinguished from the flurry of nerves unstrung by dissipation. The depression of spirits induced by dyspepsia or nervous weakness must not be taken for the depression induced by physical vice. But the percentage of ten mistakes in a hundred judgments is a fearfully small one; and these distinctions are not very difficult to learn to read.

(2) Only those rules for judging character are to be relied on which have commanded universal assent. No fanciful modern system, however much truth physiognomy or phrenology may contain, is to be leaned on with the whole weight, unless in parts which belong to what all men in all ages have admitted. Nothing less severe than this will serve as just to others, in a matter so delicate as the judgment of character; nor as safe for oneself, when one depends for preservation from being eaten up alive on this woodcraft of reading character in the forest of human souls.

In many of the vices, nothing is so much feared as exposure; and, therefore, a discussion of the signs of those vices has an important tendency to repress them, or at least drive them into the dark. The signs of the vices ought to be discussed publicly.

Throwing aside everything fanciful, enough remains to prove that no habitual vice can be permanently concealed.

1. The large signs of the vices every one can read. As to the final signs of intemperance and sensuality, carried to the most advanced stage, all men have in all ages and nations had one judgment.

2. But, in the nature of things, the fine signs must precede the large. In the nature of things, the sun cannot have reached its position at noon without passing through the position of ten o'clock, and of seven, and

of four, and of the first auroral flush. The smaller and finer signs of vice *must*, therefore, exist in the countenance. *They are there.*

3. If the signs are there, possibly they can be read. Possibly by patience and skill and practice, an expert, a medical man for instance, can read the signs much further back than ten o'clock.

4. It is universally admitted that the eye has a different expression for every different mood. It is only to make the same statement in another form to say that it has a different expression for every bad mood, as well as for every good. Every emotion—love, fear, anger—brings its peculiar light to the eye; and that light is the same for the same emotion, in all men and all places. Let any one resolve that for a month he will see no marked expression of the eye without endeavoring to ascertain what it means. *Take the lights about the meaning of which there can be no mistake. Fix these in this study as copies with which to compare other lights.* The same light means the same mood, the world around. If once you catch a marked light, and can be sure what it means, when next you catch the same light—if it can be said that the eye ever has twice precisely the same light—you may know what the second light means. If a man feels sure of the meaning of not more than ten or twenty lights, they will teach him much.

5. Complex moods exhibit themselves in complex lights. But when one has learned to read the eyes in ten or twenty lights, taken separately, he can learn to read them in combination.

6. A masked mood or a forced mood has its own peculiar light in the eye. This can be read. One of the most decisive signs of a mask in any person is that the features do not all tell the same story. Want of *consentaneous* expression in look, lips, intonation, gesture, has always been regarded as one of the most decisive signs of a mask. The attempts by the individual wearing the mask to force this consentaneous expression, destroys that sense of *ease of mood* which is one of the first signs of sincerity; and the attempt can be read.

7. Signs of the vices and signs of the virtues will often be mingled not only in the eyes, but in every part of the countenance; and difficult as it is to read simple moods, it is yet more difficult to read complex ones. But when one has learned to read simple moods, so as to recognize them wherever seen, one can learn by patience to read these moods when mingled with each other.

8. The lips are commonly admitted to have a different set for every different mood. But this is to say that they have a peculiar set for bad moods as well as good.

9. After the thirty-fifth or fortieth year, those moods which have

habitually been predominant in a man are usually marked on his countenance.

10. Like induces like. The induced mood is a test of very great significance. The mood any person concerning whom you have no strong prejudices for or against, habitually, not for once or twice, but as a plain general rule, induces in you, is an indication of the predominant mood of that person. Woman is perhaps more skilful than man in applying this test, as she is more sensitive to spiritual atmospheres.

11. *Like reads like.* The generous man reads the generous; the just man the just; and so, also, the deceitful the deceitful; and the sensual the sensual. It is, therefore, the man who has most of human nature who best reads human nature. Older reads younger. Past personal experience in the observer reads the same personal experience in the observed. You think you can easily read your younger brothers. But for most of you there are several persons in the world to whom you are the younger. It is the principle that like reads like, which is at once the most searching in its applications and the most universally admitted to be true. It is notorious that a person with a particular illness, or no more than a particular personal blemish, is peculiarly keen-sighted as to the signs of that illness or that blemish in others. *There is vice enough in the world to make men keen-sighted as to the signs of the vices.*

These principles as to the judgment of character, Mr. Cook said, were those he had been compelled to adopt for himself. They contain nothing fanciful, nothing not universally admitted, and nothing, therefore, on which a man in the collisions of life may not lean. But they are all only a reiteration of the words of Scripture, which are the words no less of human experience in history than of modern science: "Be sure your sin will find you out."

The concluding passage of Mr. Cook's address was as follows:

"There are many Saxon faces in this audience. The blue eyes, the white forehead, the blonde cheek, the fair hair, are signs of the Anglo-Saxon lineage. That race rules the world to-day. It may not always rule it. It rules it for a cause. That race has given to us Goethe and Milton and Shakespeare; and Bacon and Kant and Hamilton and Edwards; and Cromwell and Washington and Lincoln. It wrote Magna Charta, the English Constitution, the Declaration of Independence, the Constitution of the United States. It has bridged the ocean with its commerce, and traversed it with its electric wire. That race, in its German forests, was noted for nothing so much as the spotlessness of its private morals. While yet barbarian, that race, as the Roman historians state, buried the adulterer alive in the mud. The adultress was whipped through the streets. '*Non forma*,' says Tacitus, '*non aetate, non opibus, maritum invenerit*.' 'Neither beauty, nor youth, nor wealth, found her a husband. They considered,' says Tacitus, 'that there was something divine in woman, and that presaged the future, and they did not scorn her counsel and responses.' Youth were taught chivalric notions of honor. Out of this race sprang chivalry. It is this race which has proved itself, in the hurtling contests of a thousand years, both in peace and war, superior to all relaxed Italian and French tribes as the leader of all the world's civilization. The purity of the tribes in the German forests prophesied their future. The hiding of the power of the Anglo-Saxon race has been in the fact that it was at the first free from the sin of Sodom and Gomorrah. That race is passing the trial of luxury. In the German forests, our fathers, as the Romans found them, were as a race as pure as the dews the forests shook upon their heads. That race has predominated in history because free, even when barbarian, from what elsewhere has been the commonest leprosy of barbarism. It will continue to predominate if it continues free: *otherwise not*."*

Introduction to Lecture 8

Although spring weather usually brought an end to public lectures in Lynn, Cook's effective combinatin of provocative topics and dramatic oratory contined to bring out "standing room only" crowds.

In Lecture 7 Cook addressed traditional Protestant reform concerns, particularly temperance and more generally the institutions of the working class. He attacked the theater as a center of vice and moral corruption, concentrating on the working class and explicitly avoiding slurs on the upper classes. Cook argued that the upper classes had abandoned the theater for the Lyceum, the literary society, the library, the novel, and the newspaper. The theater remained, then, a center for amusement only for the "uncultivated and the vicious." French plays in particular—written, in Cook's view, for the morally inferior French population—furthered the corruption of the American working classes and offered them an alternative to a well-controlled environment dominated by the middle and upper classes. (Doubtless he would have preferred them to attend his "Theater.") Cook thus linked moral corruption with the independent institutions of amusement of

---

*The racial superiority of the Anglo-Saxons and their origins in the German forests was a strong and persistent theme among late-nineteenth-century naturalists. By linking together moral reform with naturalism, Cook built a status link between his position and the older Protestant workers. This linking of reform and racism reappears throughout much of the late-nineteenth-century reform literature. It had its antecedents in the Know-Nothing movement of the 1840s.

the working class. In this way he shifted his target from the evil environment of the factory system to the environment of the working-class community. This important shift reveals the heart of Cook's reform program: control over the new working class, rather than its freedom from exploitation.

Besides the theater, Cook also attacked the "leprous Press" or the "sewarage Press" (i.e., the popular press). Again, Cook emphasized that the problem with this press was that it was not controlled by the upper classes. Cook attacked it for its poverty and argued for its suppression, so that the better press, which in Lynn was extremely conservative, would dominate the city.

8. THE SUBVERSIVE TENDENCIES OF POPULAR CULTURE! THE THEATER AND THE "LEROUS PRESS"

Mr. Cook spoke of [sic] a few minutes on the need of a City Missionary in Lynn. There had been proposed for next Sabbath evening a gathering of all the churches in the city to consider this subject. Mr. G. P. Wilson, City Missionary of Lawrence, was to address this assembly. Mr. Wilson was one of the successful city missionaries in eastern Massachusetts. At the time of the falling of the Pemberton Mills, his services to those who suffered by that disaster in Lawrence were invaluable. A city missionary would cost Lynn, Mr. Cook thought, some two thousands dollars a year. But he would probably save the city at least half that sum every year. It was found, in the experience of city religious charities, that by timely aid to the poor, and by just discrimination between real and pretended causes of want, a most important addition can be made to the number exempted from all necessity of depending on the overseers of the poor or any other charity. In Lawrence, so true had this been found, that Mr. Wilson had been appointed to a position in the City government as disburser of the charities of Lawrence; and this as a measure of economy. It was a shame to bring forward the idea of the expense of two thousand dollars a year, as an objection to the appointment of a city missionary in a population of thirty thousand people, with twenty churches to unite in contributing this salary. But if such an objection could have weight with any, Mr. Cook called attention to the act of the city government of Lawrence in using the city missionary as an instrument of economy in public expense. It was time and high time for Lynn to have a city missionary. Of the eight or ten cities of nearly the size of Lynn this side of the Connecticut river, all but two or three had had city missionaries for years. The Young Men's Christian Association and the Women's Union, so far from objecting to the appointment of a city missionary as an encroachment on their fields, were eager to secure one. The success of the recently established Boys' Mission was one among a multitude of proofs of the need of a city mission. Independently of consultation with each other, the several pastors and churches had been found to be interested in this theme. Two important though somewhat informal and insufficiently attended meetings of the representatives of the churches, had recently pushed the subject forward to the appointment of a committee from all denominations to draft the plan of a Lynn city mission. Mr. Cook proposed to prove his interest in the enterprise of a city missionary by omitting services for one Sabbath evening at Music Hall. The twelfth of the Music Hall services would, therefore, be held April 16th. Mr. Cook most urgently invited the whole audience to be present at the city missionary meeting at the Common Street Methodist Church, next Sabbath evening.*

After devotional exercises, Mr. Cook took up the subject that had been previously announced: "Swindling Public Amusements, the Street School, and Club-Rooms in Lynn." The texts used embraced the passages in Rev. XIV, 1–2; and Proverbs IX, 10–18; especially the words: "They have no rest, day nor night, who worship the beast and his image, and whosoever receiveth the mark of his name."

"Give me a union of the Pulpit, the Parlor, the Press, and the Police," Mr. Cook began his address by saying, "and I have all I want in respect to any moral reform. But, give me a union of the Pulpit, the Parlor, and the Press, for any cause in regard to which legal enactments are expedient, and I will gain support of the Police. Give me a union of no more than the Pulpit and Parlor, and I will in time gain the Press; and, with the three, the Police. Give me only an unanimous union of the Pulpit, time enough, and a cause of importance, and I will gain the Parlor; and through the two, the Press; and through the three, the Police." It is greatly important to notice this order in which moral reform usually progresses. Pulpit and Platform, which are so far analogous in their means of influence as to be ranked together, constitute one of the four greatest powers of modern civilization. The Parlor is a second; the Press a third; Public Law a fourth. Without affirming that any one of these powers is greater than any other, it may yet be affirmed that, in the nature of things, the order of progress for a moral reform, like anti-slavery or temperance, for example, is from the first to the fourth, rather than from the fourth to the first. History shows that, in free

*The idea of a city missionary was transformed in the late 1870s into the Associated Charities, which tried to link together charity and moral reform, while at the same time hunting out the "undeserving poor."

communities, in the majority of instances for the last two hundred years, moral reform has passed from the Pulpit and Platform to the Parlor; and from these two has conquered the Press; and from these has won the recognition of Public Law.

From these circumstances, Mr. Cook went forward to draw an inference as to the importance of preserving the Pulpit and Platform from bondage. It is this natural and irreversible order of the four great means by which the interests of every class in society are protected, which makes it of such transcendent importance to every class, and, indeed, to the existence of a free civilization itself, to beware of all influences prejudicial to calm, guarded, dispassionate public discussion, in the Pulpit and Platform, of any topics touching any moral issues of society, even if tremendous interests and tremendous passions are involved.

Mr. Cook went on to illustrate this teaching of history, by speaking of the snare Slavery wove for the pulpit. Social and industrial tendrils, interwoven from the Great Lakes to the Gulf, were the meshes of the web that choked a great part of the pulpit of the North. Slavery must not be discussed, it has been said only fifteen years ago—although the day seemed a century back, by the way we had forgotten its lessons as to this bondage of public discussion!—lest these industrial and social tendrils, interwoven from the Lakes to the Gulf, should be made to rasp on each other and to bleed.

The day had not yet come in New England, but it had come in Old England when the relations of Capital and Labor, although calling out the most vigorous parliamentary legislation, weave a snare for public discussion; and for the Pulpit more than for the Platform. The meshes of the snare are not as heavy as those Slavery wove; but we are to beware, in the manufacturing centres of New England, where the distinctions between rich and poor are wide, of the weaving of even the first lines of that web.

Massachusetts has found industrial and moral questions connected with the great centres of her manufacturing populations so important as to appoint a Bureau of Labor, with heavy salaries, to investigate, under all the power of law, these problems, sure to become as complicated in New England as they have become in Old England. Already there exist in New England points connected with factory life—the employment of children in factories against law, for example—where the meshes of the snare have been woven so strongly that the officers of this Bureau of Labor publicly report to the Massachusetts Legislature that the power of State law is hardly sufficient to break the lines of the web. It is of great public importance to preserve the Pulpit of the manufacturing centres of New England from a bondage into which it is not to be charged as yet with falling; but into which the pulpit of England, from a fear of offending wealth by discussing the interests of wealth, has largely fallen.

It was in view of the extreme importance of these circumstances that Mr. Cook said that, in introducing, as he was about to do this evening, new points involving something of criticism, he wished to begin by thanking the audience, and though it the city, for the thorough manner in which it had vindicated from bondage the interests of public discussion in the pulpit of one of the most complicated of the problems arising in one of the most important of the manufacturing centres of New England, and connected with the interests of the largest trade of the United States. In view of the public importance of these considerations, Mr. Cook said: "I do not depend upon my salary for a living; but, if I had so depended; if I had wished, as I never have, for a situation in this city; if I had had a young family depending on me; and if I had had a timid wife holding me back, I should have done precisely what I have done." (Continued applause).

Mr. Cook then proceeded to discuss Swindling Public Amusements, with especial reference to the Theatre.

1. It is a fact of current history that in a majority of the theatres in the most moral cities, scenes are admitted which have on them so much of the mark of the beast that they could not be photographed without the pictures being actionable at law. Mr. Cook drew a distinction between the higher theatres and the lower; but called attention to the circumstance that the highest admitted at times scenes bearing the mark of the beast, and had done this repeatedly in Boston within four years. In proof of this assertion, Mr. Cook alluded to an article published in May, 1869, in the *Atlantic Monthly*—a most excellent authority in art, and a most liberal one in theology!—written by the accomplished editor of the *Monthly*, Mr. Howells, and running a red, crooked thunderbolt through the plays having on them the mark of the beast. "This English burlesque, this child of Mr. Offenbach's genius, and the now somewhat faded spectacular muse, flourished the past winter in three of our seven theatres for months, five, *from the highest* to the lowest, being in turn open to it." This is Boston, where the theatre is perhaps less open to criticism than in any other city in the world.

2. It is a fact of past history that the theatre, in spite of all attempts to defend it, has always had, on the whole and on the average, a bad reputation; and had this, on the whole and on the average, even in

Pagan antiquity. This permanent reputation of the theatre century after century is a fact of extraordinary significance. As one out of a score of similar illustrations, take the circumstance that in Rome, in 165 B.C., Publius Scipio Nasica, ordered a theatre, which had been partially erected, to be pulled down, exclusively on the score of public morality.

3. In view of the manner in which exceptions to this current and past reputation of the theatre are spoken of, the exceptions are themselves a proof of the rule. It is most important to recognize the exceptions. Mr. Booth is pointed out as an exception. But when it is *common* to hear exceptions spoken of *as such* in regard to any profession, *the admission is involved that the general rule is the opposite of the exceptions.* Suppose that in the medical or clerical profession it were *common* to hear men of a certain character spoken of as exceptions, what would the inference be as to the general rule?

4. *The theatre is outgrown as a mirror of the current social life and political ideas of a people, having, in both these capacities, which once gave the theatre importance, been superseded by the lyceum, the growth of modern literature, and especially by the immense increase of the power of the newspaper press.* Mr. Cook urged this point at length. In Shakespeare's day the theatre was what it could never be again, as a mirror of the current life of the people. If a stranger were to come to Boston to-day to study New England, he would find the lecture-room platforms a better mirror than the theatres of the most important phases of the current social and political New England life. It was notorious that as an instrument of political influence the theatre had been superseded by the lyceum, the newspaper press, and the growth of modern literature; and though it was not equally notorious that as a mirror of current life it had been superseded by these agencies, Mr. Cook thought that the latter proposition was now, and was likely to remain, equally true.

5. *It is safe to assert that the problem of reforming the theatre, is rendered more difficult than ever before, now that the office remaining to it is almost exclusively that of amusement, its two former offices, as mirror of the life of the people and as a political instrumentality, having been superseded.*

6. It is very important to notice that, even as a source of amusement, the theatre is now much more largely superseded *for the cultivated class,* than it was in Shakespeare's day. The theatre, even as a place of amusement, cannot be again what it was, since other forms of amusement, for both cultivated and uncultivated have increased perhaps fifty-fold in the last two hundred years. The newspaper press, the lyceum, the growth of illustrated literature, libraries, the popular use of music, are all increasing in power of amusement; and their rivalry adds

difficulty to any attempt by the theatre to succeed as a place of amusement; and it must succeed as that, or not at all.

7. *Amusement is now so open elsewhere to the cultivated that it is found that a theatre managed according to their tastes as a place of amusement does not pay the expense necessary to satisfy a cultivated taste.*

8. The temptation to address, in the theatre, the tastes of the uncultivated and the vicious, is, therefore, extremely great; but it is a temptation arising from circumstances of permanent and increasing influence in modern civilization.

9. In European society, especially in the French city populations, the condition of the mass of the people, is politically, socially, and intellectually, so different from the condition of American society, that the former can be amused by what is not at all adapted to the latter. *We are superior to the French plays.* But it is from abroad that the plays which do most to corrupt our cities come; and, instead of being admired as foreign, they ought to be criticised as such. *Theatrical amusements fitted to satisfy the mass of a European population, are, because of that fitness, inferior to the demands of an American population.*

10. The low theatres are a host, and the better only a handful, and the latter have much less influence than the former. But of the latter it must be said that to-day, in Boston, where the purest theatre of the world exists, enough of the mark of the beast is admitted into the plays to make it difficult for a man to go in at the doors of the theatre without stooping; and into the low theatres a man cannot go except on all-fours.

Dr. Holmes remarks that every man leads or is led by something that goes on all-fours. It may be added, that if the human race is ever to find a paradise, it will not enter it on all-fours.

Mr. Cook then proceeded to discuss the Street School, with especial reference to the corrupt illustrated popular press. This he termed the Leprous Press—the Savage Press.

1. If it must be acknowledged that its force is increasing, it must be admitted also that the force of the better press is vastly increasing.

2. Europeans, especially German and English travellers, point to the failure of our city governments to clear the street windows of the leprous and sewerage press, as a proof of the inferiority of democracy as a form of government. Boston and New York allow what would not be allowed in London.

3. The offices from which most of these sheets emanate are usually of the shabbiest and lowest kind. Mr. Cook described the office of one of the leprous sheets of Boston he had visited—four broken panes in the front door, a hall full of filth and broken furniture, and the editorial

room only a small space cleared in an apartment filled elsewhere as a storeroom of furniture, and containing nothing belonging to the editors that could not have been packed up in an hour. In New York he had seen a basement-room used for similar purposes where a tar-can was an ornament on the walls, and the only counter two boards laid on two barrels. The offices are like the Arab's tent, capable of being packed up at the shortest notice; and this is one reason why the police have difficulty with them.

4. It is worth much to drive these papers into such a position that they can be read only on the sly; and this, a public statement of their character helps to do.

5. Mr. Cook took the responsibility of advising the public not to patronize, for anything whatever, newspaper dealers in the leprous press.

The speaker referred to the habit of evening walking on the street, somewhat characteristic of this city, with its beautiful scenery close at hand, and pointed out that the perils connected with that habit have many illustrations elsewhere.

It was Mr. Cook's intention to have spoken on the Club-room; but he had addressed the audience, wholly without notes, for the full hour, and would take up that topic at the next service. He had been with two policemen through two of the club-rooms of the city. He had, of course, exceptions to make as to social and literary clubs. He knew of one club that did *not* open Sundays. But, as to the mass of the club-rooms, they were places where Satan gave his degree of LL.D. What does that LL.D. mean? Liquor and Locked Doors. (Applause.) — *Lynn Semi-Weekly Reporter,* April 5, 1871.

INTRODUCTION TO LECTURE 9

Even after two months Cook could fill all the seats in the Music Hall with a hundred or more eager listeners standing throughout his 2¹/₂-hour service. After pleading with his audience to support a city mission (which could not in Lynn depend upon corporate support as it did in Lawrence), Cook launched into an attack on pubs and club rooms. Not only did they offer alcohol, against the laws of the state, but—of equal importance to Cook—they were a center of political power for the working classes. "Clubs increase in power with the increase of the power of cities." Cook claimed to have no objection in principle to the club rooms of the "better sort," but said that those club rooms of the lower classes were centers of corruption, poorly furnished, with copies of popular press on the tables. In effect, Cook attacked these clubs because they were working-class institutions.

In dealing with the problem of the growing power of the urban working class, Cook argued for the suppression of local democracy. Couching his argument in terms of the need for temperance reform, Cook looked to greater state law enforcement and an increase of the state police. In doing so, he linked his concern for more control and order with the desire of the manufacturing classes for a police structure beyond the control of the local community. In Lynn and elsewhere, local elections often returned police chiefs sympathetic to unions and ultimately to strikers. Thus, social control for reform became social control over the working class. Cook saw the plan for a state police as one of the best solutions yet invented for the problem of the perishing and dangerous classes of the city. In addition to removing the local community from power, it also, he asserted, gave greater power to that section of the state dominated by Protestant Anglo-Saxons.

Cook looked to those who shared his own background for support in the new urban industrial world. "Unless the portions of New York above the highlands of the Hudson (rural Protestant New York) helped to rule the part below the highlands, (urban areas with large numbers of Catholic immigrants) the latter would hardly be governable except by martial law."

By Lecture 9 Cook's concern for reaching the working class with factory reform had become a call for greater control over the working class by the state, a state controlled by the upper and middle classes. Cook's reforms, which initially generated so much hostility from manufacturers, had reached the point of rejecting sympathy for workers and instead called for greater domination over them.

9. POLITICS AND SOCIAL CONTROL

I. *Need for Temperance Legislation*

1. "Standing in one of the open squares of this city last evening with a policeman," said Mr. Cook, "I said: 'There is a white horse in the center of the square. If you stood where that horse stands, into how many places where liquor is illegally sold could you throw a stone?' The policeman, a cautious man, replied, looking about the square: 'One, two, three—seven—ten—twelve or fifteen, at least.'" The day might come yet, in the future of this city, when, unless public sentiment in a larger population is made a police behind the police, ten or fifteen such squares may be open within hearing of the waves of Massachusetts Bay! But the evil one such square and all it represents can do is not easily calculated.

2. It is common for the best portions of the Pulpit and Parlor and

Press, in our cities, to complain of the inefficiency of the Police in executing Temperance Laws.

3. It is also common, in our cities, for the Police to complain that there is no public sentiment to justify them in the execution of Temperance Laws; that is, they complain of the Pulpit, Parlor, and Press for not awakening such sentiment. Go to the Pulpits and Parlors, and you find complaints made of the City Marshals and Chiefs of Police; go to the City Marshals and Chiefs of Police, and you find complaint made of the Pulpits and Parlors.

4. Both these sets of complaints are just. As a general rule, it is true that the Police are right in their complaints of the Pulpit, Parlor, and Press; and the Pulpit, Parlor, and Press right in their complaints of the Police.

5. It is impossible for the Police alone to secure the right condition of a great city in respect to Temperance or any other moral reform; and it is also impossible for the Pulpit, Parlor, and Press, taken without the aid of the Police, to secure that right condition.

6. The two sets of ideas represented in these complaints must, therefore, recognize each the just claims of the other, and clasp hands together under the neck of the moral difficulties always arising in crowded centres of population, or the great problem of the right management of cities will never be solved.

7. The scheme of State Police, or a constabulary representing the whole State, and executing the temperance laws of the State, unites, perhaps better than any other plan, these two sets of ideas; for it brings the vigorous temperance sentiment of the rural portions of a State to the support of the less vigorous temperance sentiment of the cities. Unless the portions of New York above the Highlands of the Hudson helped to rule the part below the Highlands, the latter would hardly be governable, except by martial law. The plan of a State Police is one of the best solutions yet invented for the problem of the perishing and dangerous classes in cities.

8. There is nothing undemocratic in the plan of a State Police. The republican plan of government is, that the executive should be coordinated in the sphere of its power with the legislation and the judiciary. The legislative power makes laws, including temperance laws, for all the State. The executive power should execute the laws, including temperance laws, for all the State. This is the true theory of republican institutions, and was the practice in Massachusetts until about fifty years ago.

9. It follows from the preceding propositions, and has now been

proved by experience, that a State Prohibitory Law, enforced by a State Police, brings, better than any other plan, the force of the better parts of a State to the aid of the worse. Mr. Cook declared himself in favor of Prohibition.

10. In the most unfortunately situated cities, however, taken without the aid of any public sentiment outside of themselves, there are tides of temperance sentiment enough seated in the churches and parlors to make a police behind the police, if the Pulpits and Press would only give that sentiment adequate expression.

11. Massachusetts is now, in respect to temperance legal enactments, under what may be called the system of Local Option. Each town has its option whether it will permit the sale of the malt liquors, or not. This city has, at present, a very good set of temperance enactments. But several cities in Eastern Massachusetts have recently been turned against temperance by small majorities in municipal elections; and this with the most ruinous results.

12. *While the system of Local Option prevails in temperance legislation, it is plain that great responsibility rests on the local Pulpit, Parlor, and Press.* On the grounds of these propositions, Mr. Cook made an appeal to the Pulpit, Parlor, and Press of the city to unite in making public sentiment a police behind the police to aid the police to shut the open bars.

II. *Club-Rooms*

1. It is important to notice, in cities, that middle ground which exists between respectability, on the one hand, and action which the police can touch, on the other. Men are divided not only into the standing and fallen. There is a third class—the *falling*. This is found in this middle ground oftener than elsewhere. It is peculiarly the province of the Pulpit and Parlor to study this middle ground.

2. Club-rooms in cities occupy, as a mass, this middle ground; although the better of them rise into the region of respectability, and the lowest sink into the region of illegality, and fall into the hands of police law.

3. Clubs increase in power with the increase of the power of cities. This is true of the political and literary and social clubs, on the one hand, as well as of the drinking and gambling clubs, on the other. Wendell Phillips complains that Massachusetts is ruled politically by Boston Clubs; and he was fortunate in being able in a recent political campaign to put one of those clubs into the pillory.

4. When severe temperance legislation is executed in cities, the lower class of club-rooms blossom. Many of the club-rooms of this city had their origin at the time the Prohibitory Law was thoroughly executed here. This is no argument against a Prohibitory Law; but it is an indication that drinking is an essential object with the lower class of club-rooms.

5. The Police in this city often find places that are in reality dram-shops, defended, when brought before the city courts, on the plea by the lawyers that they are club-rooms. This is another indication of the true character of the lower class of these places.

6. Mr. Cook said he had studied the club-rooms of Lynn by the aid of the police. He found, on inquiry of the proper officers, that in Lynn, as in larger cities, it was not unusual or regarded in any sense improper for persons wishing to study the moral condition of the population to avail themselves of the aid of the police; and he paid a high compliment to the police for the courtesy and fulness of the aid they give in such a study of the city. He had been, with company from the police, through four establishments, one of which was one of the worst gambling-rooms in the city, another a club-room of the better class, and two which were called specimens of the club-rooms of the worst class. He had gone in his usual dress without disguise; and in two of the club-rooms had had quite full and always courteous conversations with persons present in them; and he should speak from personal observation, as well as from the information of the police.

7. In the places he had visited, and which were called specimens of the worst class of club-rooms, he found the outer doors locked and provided with a small window through which any who applied for admission, and especially the policemen, were observed from within, before being admitted. It was useless to set up the claim that this arrangement was intended solely to keep out persons not members of the club. *The police found their investigations in these rooms barred by the windows and the locked doors.* When a policeman applies for admission, a delay usually occurs, long enough for any evidence of illegal liquor-selling or gambling that may be going on within, to be put out of sight. "If you are all right, why do you not admit us without so much delay?" the police significantly asked twice in one of the rooms. "We are all right," was the answer. In the cases he had observed, Mr. Cook found nothing attractive, but everything shabby, about the rooms. In each case, a bar-room and an adjoining sitting-room made up the establishment. The places are fitted up with no taste, and one of them was so shabby

and repulsive that Mr. Cook said he came out of it thankful that he had a clean pillow on which to lay his head. The floor was filthy; the walls and windows dirty; the table bare; and all the furniture in the room would not have sold at auction for fifteen dollars. There was one little colored print, of no significance, on the walls; a cask with a faucet (probably containing water!) on the floor near a closet and a bar. In another room he saw three of the most leprous illustrated newspapers on the bare table; and the pictures on the walls were in part of the same class with those in the papers, and in part of bosing [sic] and racing scenes. It was the general rule in the city, as he had been informed by the police, that the club-rooms of the lower class are shabby and repulsive places. But they are frequented from morning to night, and till late at night; and most of them keep open on Sundays. The police estimate that there are at present some thirty or thirty-five club-rooms of this class in the city.

8. Where is the money in club-rooms made? Mr. Cook said he regarded this a test question in determining their true character. He had put this question everywhere; and had concurrent information, both from the police and those [with] whom he had conversed within the club-rooms, that the money is made from the bar and from toll on the table. When a person sits down at a club-room table at a game, it is customary to charge a small sum—perhaps twenty cents—for a sitting; and the money made by the managers of club-rooms is from the bar and from this toll on the games. It used to be said of John Quincy Adams, when in Congress, that he had a carnivorous instinct for the jugular vein and carotid artery of an argument. Mr. Cook regarded the fact that the club-room managers make their money from their bars and the toll on the tables as the jugular vein and carotid artery of the proof that, whatever may be said of the character of these places as opened for social intercourse or amusement, their essential business is gambling and drinking.

9. When the current sets all one way, in any social gathering, the effect of putting oneself into that current is always of a very marked kind. In a prayer-meeting, not of the hypocritical sort, the current sets all one way; and this toward virtue. This is the secret of the power of such a meeting, and is one reason why some men are so shy of putting themselves into that current. But, in a club-room of the lower class, the central currents are gambling and drinking; and these draw in gradually the side swirls of mere social intercourse or good fellowship, until it may be said that the current all sets one way, and that toward the

direction the central current takes. This is the secret of the influence of putting oneself into that current. The thoroughly equipped low club-room of a great city is a prayer meeting of the Devil's Church.

10. Those who, at any age, are under the power of bad habits, and the young, are the two classes most injured among the membership of club-rooms; and both these classes are most numerously represented in that membership. It is not an unknown circumstance for very old persons to belong to club-rooms. The young have so much representation in them that Mr. Cook found that teachers exhibit high interest in the subject. The High School of this city is a gem, and this even on the Massachusetts coast, more irradiated by the gems of the schools than any other coast in the world. The princely Principal of the school, who knows the city well, is not without the information as to club-rooms needed to bar out their influences from the first.

11. The class of clubs meeting for political, social, or literary purposes, Mr. Cook said he did not intend to discuss. He had visited one of the clubs of this class, conversed with its members, and read its constitution, which contained provisions, which the police believed were thoroughly executed, against all liquor on the premises, and against opening on Sundays. He saw nothing in any part of club-life, however, which could afford any adequate reason why a busy man, with but a few hours to devote to his family each day, should give four, three or two evenings, or even one evening a week, regularly, to a club. (Applause.)

12. In the low club-rooms, the Sabbath is often the worst day of the week.

III. *Gambling Rooms*

1. Arrangements for blockading or retarding the coming in of the police were visible enough at the entrance of the gambling-room, as well as at the entrance of the club-rooms.

2. Mr. Cook described the gambling-room he had visited, and a room connected with it, as of the shabbiest and forlornest character; and the furniture in the gambling-room, aside from a rough table, as not worth ten dollars.

3. And as yet, in this room, gambling of the most thorough sort, the police has [sic] reason enough to believe, was carried on. It did not require a long apprenticeship to acquire skill enough to shake four small flattened sea-shells, called props, like dice in the hand; and determine a game by the shells coming, four or two, the same side up,

and making a *neck;* or three one side up and one the other side up, and making an *out.*

IV. *Dwelling-House Drinking Parties*

1. When the Catholic clergy of Boston were called before the Massachusetts Legislature, to testify in the License Hearings conducted by Governor Andrew and President Miner in 1867, they testified in the strongest terms that one of the most deadly evils they met in the population they were called most to study, was the sale of liquors in private dwelling-houses. They represented that there were whole streets and squares of dwelling-houses, especially among the population of foreign descent, where the whole moral ground was as springy with these sales as a marsh is with rills. They condemned this habit of the population as an evil of the first magnitude; and as not altogether confined to the foreign population.

2. Mr. Cook said that he knew a street in this city where he had reason, from information received from the police, to believe that liquor is sold in every third dwelling-house.

3. Pass through such a street on the Sabbath, and although no outward disorder may be seen, it is common to find, sometimes on one street, five or six dwelling-house Sabbath drinking parties. Ten or fifteen persons in some back room of a dwelling-house are gathered about a supply of liquor, drinking. When the police appears [sic], the group scatters, some up stairs, some to the closets, some to the cellars.

4. The police assert that they had rather have four open bars than one dwelling-house drinking hole.—*Lynn Semi-Weekly Reporter,* April 22, 1871.

INTRODUCTION TO LECTURE 10

On May 2, 1871, the Reverend Joseph Cook delivered his last lecture in Lynn. As had been the case in his previous lectures he filled the Hall. In this lecture, which he entitled, "Farewell Discourse in Lynn," Cook recounted the major points he had made during the earlier lectures. He emphasized the importance of the reforms he had suggested in terms of the growing change occurring throughout the nation. "The Atlantic slope of New England . . . rushes beneath factory wheels." He argued that unless New England woke up to the reforms he suggested, the "industrial conditions of Old England" would overtake New England and soon the nation. But Cook stated confidently that something had already been done. Through his dramatic action, "a subtile and large evil has been exposed," "remedies for it have been suggested," "and public sentiment has been carried overwhelmingly in favor of those remedies."

Cook fulfilled the expectations of his sponsors. *He brought the church into the city limelight.* By presenting himself and the church as crusaders for reform apart from both labor and capital he staked out a role for the church that neither challenged the structure of nineteenth-century industrial capitalism nor appeared to endorse it. *In doing this he accomplished much—although considerably less than he would have had his audience believe.*

10: FAREWELL AND HARBINGER FOR THE FUTURE

Changes in New England in the Last Fifty Years

When Edmund Burke was a young man he wrote a letter to a friend, stating that he had a plan of going to America for life; and this because the Western Continent was sure to be the seat of a great nation; was in the infancy of great changes; and was, therefore, a field in which effort put forth early would have usefulness on a great scale. New England is to-day in the infancy of great changes. It may be that if Edmund Burke were alive he would think the new opportunity of usefulness not inferior to the old.

1. The population of the manufacturing districts of New England is increasing with extraordinary rapidity.

It is the recommendation of Demosthenes that all speeches should begin with an incontrovertible proposition. It is incontrovertible that this city, as one manufacturing centre in New England, has passed through great changes in the last twenty years. I should have exhibited but a callous sensitiveness to the grave responsibilities of public speech, if I could have forgotten for an instant, in discussing the future of this city, that in the last twenty years your population has doubled, the value of the products of your chief industry trebled, and the amount of your taxable property quadrupled. It is fabled by the poets that whoever will put his ear to the ground in the thifty and jubilant days of that season of the year we are now entering, may hear the noise of growing things. Lynn is a meadow slope on which the sun of secular prosperity has shone so brightly for the last twenty years that there is hardly a sod of it on which you can put your ear without hearing the sound of growing things.

But, is this growth a merely local phenomenon? The last census has an astonishing answer to make. The growth is characteristic of nearly every manufacturing centre in Eastern Massachusetts; and I had almost said of every such centre from Long Island Sound to the White Mountains, and from Cape Cod to the Berkshire Hills.

Take the seven cities on the Merrimac River. I often hand [sic] in imagination above that stream as the best emblem of the life of Eastern New England. Child of the White Mountains and of the Pemigewasset, the Merrimac rushes past the innumerable spindles of seven cities to the sea—Concord, Manchester, Nashua, Lowell, Lawrence, Haverhill, and Newburyport—doing more work than any other river of its size in the world; and emblematic from source to mouth of the industrial life of the Atlantic slope of New England, which more and more rushes beneath factory wheels through all its vexed course from its source in the mountains to its home in the ocean. These seven cities, in the last twenty years, have, in the aggregate, more than doubled in wealth and population. Lawrence has grown from a pasture to a princely manufacturing centre within twenty years.

Draw a line north and south cutting the population of Massachusetts in halves and through what point does it now pass? Draw another east and west, cutting the population in halves, and where does that line fall? The intersection of the two lines is the centre of population. The centre of territory is within the limits of the city of Worcester, on the easterly side, near Lake Quinsagamon. But where is the centre of population? Is it Framingham? Is it Lake Cochituate? The north and south line which cuts the population of Massachusetts in halves passes easterly of a point midway between Harvard University and the west end of West Boston Bridge. The east and west line dividing the population into equal portions passes through the South Boston end of the Federal Street Bridge. The two lines intersect at a point not two miles west of the State House. This, according to the State documents, was the centre of population in 1865. [Abstract of the Census of 1865, with Remarks on the same and Supplementary Tables, Prepared under the direction of Oliver Warner, Secretary of the Commonwealth, p. 274.] The centralization of wealth is even more remarkable than that of the population. The census everywhere reveals the fact that, through the aid of the wonderful increase of all means of intercommunication, the change which is constantly givin greater and greater power to cities, this added weight of the Atlantic slope of the State is chiefly an effect of the extraordinary growth of the manufacturing centres of Eastern Massachusetts. Of these, Boston itself is one. I must be pardoned for considering it a suggestive circumstance that, in spite of the remarkable advances of Central and Western Massachusetts, the circumscribing line drawn from the State House, and containing half the population of the Commonwealth, has contracted its radius ten miles in fifty years. All Eastern Massachusetts is a factory. In 1865, more than one half of the population of Massachusetts, seven tenths of the personal property, and two thirds of the real estate, were situated within twenty-five miles of the State House at Boston. [Ibid. p. 275.] In the five years since these astonishing estimates were made, your city has increased thirty-six percent in population. But Lawrence has increased thirty-two in the same time; Lowell has increased thirty-one; Haverhill, nineteen and Fall River forty.

Here is the incoming of an Atlantic tide. It is the roar of the industrial conditions of Old England coming into New England. I have lived for a year within hearing of the roar of the ocean. I have looked daily upon the coming in of the vast tides. It is little to say that I profess to have lived also within hearing of the roar of the human ocean which beats on the Atlantic slope of New England; and have looked daily upon the coming in of these vast tides. Imagine the magnificent coast-line from Newfoundland to New York beaten in all its coves and headland by incoming Atlantic waves. A feeble occupation this, compared with imagining the same coast, beaten, as it is, in all its coves and headlands, and likely to be beaten more and more furiously as the years pass, by these incoming human tides, and more and more complicated industrial conditions. Not discuss these conditions! Not secure the best life that can be secured for millions whose future is now being largely determined by the precedents which are to be set in the period of transition New England is passing! Not turn public discussion and legislation early to the solution of problems more vital than any others in the secular life of New England, and sure to become more and more complicated as the tides rise higher! He who says this is likely to be as little regarded as the rattling of rushes before the coming in of an Atlantic surge. (Applause.)

2. It is notorious that, while the population of the manufacturing centres of New England is increasing with extraordinary rapidity, that of the agricultural and commercial districts is fluctuating, and, in many cases, on the decrease.

3. The distinctions between rich and poor are becoming wider in the manufacturing district.

(1) This is partly the unavoidable result of the growth of the power of capital. (2) It is in part the consequence of the massing of men in cities, as distinct from small towns. (3) It is in part the natural effect of the organization of manufacturing industry in great corporations on the one hand, and an operative population on the other. (4) It is also in

large measure the result of the fact that in the manufacturing districts of New England, a vastly greater proportion of the population is now of foreign descent than fifty years ago.

For nearly a century and a half the people of New England, consisting in 1640 of only about 4,000 families of 20,000 persons, multiplied on their own soil in remarkable seclusion from other communities. Bancroft points out that after the first fifteen years following the landing of the Pilgrims, there was never any considerable increase from England. Palfrey makes prominent the circumstance that it is chiefly within the last forty years that the foreigners have come. It is not true to say that New England is beoming New Ireland. But it is hardly epigrammatic to say that manufacturing New England is becoming New Ireland. Out of every hundred of the population, the number of foreign born was in 1865 in Lowell, 30; in Fall River, 31; in Boston, 34; in Lawrence, 42. [Census of Massachusetts for 1865, Abstract of, p. 298.]

4. As soon as our population is thick enough, large parts of the industrial difficulties of Old England are likely, in spite of American Institutions, to arise in New England.

It is not safe to trust the action of democratic institutions to solve the problems which a monarchy as free as England has been unable to solve. What is the ministry in Great Britain but a committee of Parliament, obliged to lay down its power whenever it cannot command the support of a majority? There is no such difference between American and English political institutions, as will prevent the larger part of the questions that trouble the industrial relations of England from crossing the Atlantic. We have, indeed, no aristocracy based on blood. But it is notorious that, in spite of every feudal inheritance in English social and political life, the aristocracy based on land and manufactures and other forms of wealth has more power in England to-day than that based on hereditary descent.

5. The sooner New England begins to prepare remedies for its industrial difficulties the better.

(1) The legislation of England for a hundred years has demonstrated the necessity of rectifying abuses in manufacturing centres by investigations conducted under the authority of law. (2) The best literature of England for the last hundred years turns on no points more vital than the condition of the poor and the relations of employers and employed. (3) I maintain that it is greatly to the honor of Massachusetts to have organized, first of all the States, a Bureau of Labor.

These five are plain, large, and incontrovertible propositions. I confess that I am moved by them to think that, while all old duties remain as sacred as ever, and while some old duties are becoming more sacred than ever,

> "New occasions teach new duties, we ourselves must Pilgrims be,
> Launch our Mayflowers, and steer boldly through the desperate winter sea."

The changes in New England in the last fifty years! They expose by more than glimpses new duties thrown upon the churches, the press, the platform, the parlors and the workrooms of New England. A very dull and unpoetic fact, it may seem, that New England is inevitably to be a factory. It is one already. Plymouth Rock began the first New England. Shall it be the corner-stone of the second? Goethe listened to the spindles of Manchester and said, with profound meaning, that he thought theirs the most suggestively poetic sound of the century. He foresaw the future industrial conditions of the cities of the world, and yearned for the unborn ten thousand times ten thousand for whom that sound was a prophetic note. But all men have not Goethe's ears. When you and I are no longer in the world, the problem of the future of New England will be how to make Plymouth Rock the corner-stone of a factory. Who are the masons that shall lay that jagged and fundamental Rock smooth with the other stones of the wall? And if the lines of the Rock and of the other stones of the wall should not be the same, shall the other stones be hewn, or Plymouth Rock to [*sic*] be hewn, to bring out the line? God send us no future into which Plymouth Rock cannot be built unhewn! But how to build that Rock into the complicated lines of the industrial relations of the future of the cities with which New England is to be crowded? How to make Plymouth Rock the corner-stone of a factory? I admit that the question, except to Goethe's ears, has almost the sound of sacrilege. But the Sphinx of current history, daughter of Typhon and Chimaera as was the Sphinx of old, already asks it in whispers; will ask it in the next generation in bold speech; and in the next century with the voice of many waters; and the penalties of not answering are not likely to be inconsiderable!

Review of the Winter

Some weeks ago I said I felt like Bismark in Paris. It was a facetious remark. But I may now make one of more significance. I feel like Bismark in Paris.* (Applause.) Three important results have been accomplished:

*On March 3, 1871, German troops marched into Paris. Like many reformers of the day, Cook saw the Germans under Bismarck as conservative moderates and the French as an unruly inferior mob.

1. A subtle and large evil has been exposed;
2. Remedies for it have been suggested;
3. Public sentiment has been carried overwhelmingly in favor of those remedies.

For any who wish an argument for the two measures of Factory Reform which have been recommended, I offer the fact that in this city, where the subject is better understood than it can be elsewhere, local public sentiment has overwhelmingly favored those measures.

Thucydides and Talleyrand, though as widely separated in character as in time, both advise that those who would deal with the pubic usefully or successfully should practice entire freedom from indirection. The secret of securing attention, as well as of speaking usefully, is to say the thing that needs to be said.

There are several facts of public notoriety here which are now matters of the past. I judge that the past is not likely to be reversed.

1. It has now been my fortune to speak in Music Hall for more than a quarter of a year. It is only two weeks less than a third of a year since the first of the Music Hall Services.

2. In January, I made here certain very damaging charges concerning the condition of your chief industry.

3. The charges were such that beyond doubt I should have been advised, if I had consulted beforehand with any one not wise as a serpent but harmless as a dove, not to present them.

4. So damaging were the charges and so public and unequivocal was their presentation, that, if they had been untrue, or if they had contained substantial exaggeration, I should have been made the most unpopular man in public life in this city, and months ago have been hissed off this platform.

5. I have not been hissed off the platform. I am saying nothing of the necessity of repressing applause here night after night for a quarter of a year; nor of a deliberate request from the class said to have been slandered, for the continuance of the meetings; nor of scores of other indications. In a gathering of some sixty-five operatives in this city last winter, not long after the topic of the factories had been brought to public attention, a vote was taken on the question of the advisability of the separation of the sexes. Two speeches were made against the measure; and the vote stood for it, sixty-three to two. The assertion that the proportion of these figures to each other fairly represents the present sentiment of the fifteen thousand working people here, I make no use of, except to say that it comes to me from an exceedingly large number of the most respectable sources, and that no counterbalancing

evidence reaches me. It is not consonant with the rules of local Crispin lodges* to act on certain themes without a kind of concurrent action or permission from national or international lodges; otherwise, resolutions which have been twice prepared by working men to be brought before the local lodges here on this theme, would have been passed. I notice that the admirable Report of the Massachusetts Bureau of Labor, published but a few days since for the use of the Legislature, has a passage comparing the moral perils of the old and new system of your chief industry; and bases an inference that the perils of the latter are the greater, on the fluctuations of the business, the very point urged three months since in this Hall. These and many other similar facts it is not necessary to bring into employment. It is enough to say simply that I have not been hissed off the platform. Every man of sense who heard what I said in January knows that I should have been, if I had not spoken substantially without exaggeration. As to the applause, petition, and other indications of local sentiment, they mean as much as they would on the other side. How much is that? As much as they would on the other side, if that side had ever received them. (Applause.) When poor John Sterling, Thomas Carlyle's friend, after a life tossed with scepticism, lay dying, he said: "Bring me the Bible I used to use in visits among the cottages at Herstmonceaux," and laid his head on it, as if in rest from all his tossing. I will remember these two hundred signatures of working men, as John Sterling remembered the Bible used among the cottages at Herstmonceaux.

6. Nearly four months have now passed. There has been abundant time for sentiment to become calm and intelligent. Photograph public sentiment as it stood two months ago. It was overwhelmingly on the right side; but it would have been unfair to take the picture to fix the record then. The picture was too near and would have been blurred. Take the photograph to fix the record two years hence, when all the facts will not be fresh in memory, and the picture would be too dim. Now is the time to take the photograph to fix the record. There has been no especial excitement in the city for the last month.

The photograph is fixed by these six propositions. I recite them not for my own sake, but as an incontrovertible indication of local public sentiment. The propositions are all matters utterly undeniable. They are such as a stranger looking on from outside, might be sure of. But whoever will run his eye along the six, and take their trend, will see that

---

*The Knights of St. Crispin were trade unionists in the shoe industry. They were quite active in Lynn in the early 1870s, but were weakened by loss of strikers in 1872.

an inference follows from them as to the nature of local public sentiment which I to-night add to all the arguments I have heretofore
advanced.

And now it is my duty to thank this city, which is dear to me, and will
continue to be dear, as are the ruddy drops that visit a glad heart. You
have not been misled. You have not been intimidated. There are many
ways in which Capital may act as a Ku Klux Klan. Capitalists range all
the way from the George Peabodys to the James Fisks.* Years ago there
came into classic use in this commonwealth the significant word gerrymandered. To divide a state into political districts in such a manner as to
favor a particular political party, was a scheme which, under Elbridge
Gerry's administration, was forever put into the pillory by that single
word. I have met, in one of the most scholarly publications of Boston,
the word gymfiscation. It has as good a right to become a part of the
language as the word gerrymandered. You are yet a young city. You
have yet but a comparatively small population. I say and beg you to
notice that I say that I think you have no one or two, or any other
number, as corporations or as individuals, near, or nigh to near, to that
rank of capitalists which the James Fisks represent at the end of the
scale opposite to the George Peabodys at the other. But you will have
them in the future. Let me beseech you to remember that all your
difficulties will assuredly increase with a more crowded population. I
am not thinking of your past. I am thinking of your future. Charles
Dickens regarded it as a peculiar vice of American cities that they are
managed almost exclusively by local capitalists. In his celebrated American Notes he pointed this out as the peculiar shame of Americans. As I
hope the city will never be politically gerrymandered, so I hope New
Lynn will never be gymfiscated. I thank the singers. I thank the newspapers. I thank the public sentiment of the churches.

And now, to my own church, God send the spotless robes and the
queenly spirit of a Bride of Christ, and enable her to carry them
untarnished through all the dusty ways of the future of this city. My
whole motive for a year, and a more solemn one could not lie upon
man, has been to do my whole duty as a minister of a church exposed to
the fierce temptations of a crowded population in a manufacturing
centre. I was resolved that the church should be put on its knees neither
to Labor on the one hand, not to Capital on the other, nor to City Vices

*Peabody was a well-known merchant and philanthropist who gave money to various
educational and cultural causes and to maintain confidence overseas in the American
economy. Fisk was a stock speculator whose speculations led to the ruin of hundreds
during the Black Friday crash of 1869.

in any form; but on its knees only to Christ. The topics selected by me in this Hall have, for evident reasons, been off the range of my usual courses of public remark. It has been my fortune to pass the last three years almost exclusively in speaking from point to point of New England in revivals. In the first half of the year which I have passed in this city, there was a revival in the church. This was in the heat of summer; and it was my plan to fill the whole winter with the most severe labor in revival. Some fourteen had united with the church by profession of faith. But on Christmas night the church edifice was burned. That event of necessity changed the plan of the winter. Although all the churches of the city held out their arms full of generosity to us; and although one of them, with a generosity which it will take long to repay, has held us in its arms every Sabbath since our calamity, it was found, after careful inquiry, that there was no place open to the church where Sabbath evening devotional meetings could be conveniently held. The devotional meetings had exhibited, up to the last, the best state; had more than trebled in size; and it was my intention that you should have done severe work in them for the whole winter. We were driven to this Hall. When the fire took place and we came here, the church was lifted for half of each Sabbath from the position of a wax taper in one parlor at West Lynn to that of a watchtower for the whole city. I thank the church for the resolution it passed unanimously after my address of January 22, when public opposition was offered to the performance of its plain duty. You understood perfectly, when you passed your resolution, that a pulpit which is allowed by the parish that owns it to be plastered over with directions from outside the parish, or whittled by knives not sharpened on the foundation stone Jesus Christ, becomes such a symbol that it may be difficult to find a man to stand behind the whittled thing. I was told in Boston the other day by a lawyer, that matters had been carried so far that two and perhaps more parties here owed their freedom from the clutches of the law exclusively to my forbearance. I have never replied to attack on myself. When your interests have been involved, when public interests of the city have been involved, when the freedom of public discussion has been involved, I have made reply. God send you in your new church edifice a revival of that deep and calm kind which was going forward in the old when the flames came; and may the increase of that religious thoughtfulness and enthusiasm fill the new temple as the flames filled the old. God send you a minister whom no one can vex, or cajole, or browbeat, or outwit. I love this church; and, when I lie dying, I will remember that we labored together for the poor. And now my face is toward Eurpoe. When from the deck of the steamer I look toward Lynn from Massachusetts Bay, as the gates of the ocean draw near, the multitudinous waves shall not be more abounding than the good I will wish you and this city, until we meet, when the heavens are no more. The supreme duty is to follow the Pillar of Fire.

A letter has been placed in my hands which I will read and answer here in the serious presence of this assembly.

Lynn, April 29, 1871

Rev. Joseph Cook:

Dear Friend and Pastor: Please accept this picture and these books from a few of your friends in the First Congregational Church and Society in Lynn, who, painfully conscious of the inadequacy of words, or of any token to express the sentiments of high regard which they entertain for you personally, and for the labors you have performed in the endeavor to promote their eternal welfare and that of others, present them to you, that in the future they may remind you of those who desire not to be forgotten yet dare not presume that, in the eventful and eminently useful life which they anticipate for you, they shall preseve a place in your memory without something constantly near you to represent each of them, and to say for each, "Remember me."

> Mr. and Mrs. J. F. Patten,
> Mr. and Mrs. G. H. Chadwell,
> Mr. and Mrs. Chas. E. Ashcroft,
> Mr. George F. Hosmer,
> *Committee*

On returning yesterday afternoon from the crowded delight of finishing a tour of two hundred calls in the church and society, I was met at my rooms by the entire surprise of your costly and most beautiful gifts: a magnificent picture, called "The Sealers Crushed by the Icebergs," and valued at ninety dollars; the volumes entitled "The Circle of the Sciences," valued at twenty-five dollars; and "The English Hexapla," in the most valuable of the English editions, valued at twenty dollars. I have received private assurances that the plan of making these gifts was of the most spontaneous kind both in conception and in execution.

I can bear opposition; but it is not so easy to bear kindness. I confess that I felt unmanned by this blow; and do not think that I shall soon recover from it!

A city church is either the best or the worst place to grow Christians in. If, in a crowded population, where the temptations of a church are the fiercest, these are resisted, the church becomes strong in proportion to the fierceness of its temptations. But, if they are not resisted, it is a wholly familiar teaching of Church History as well as of the Scriptures, that a church may become one of the most withered, juiceless and jejune of all the beads of growth on God's vine. Your gifts, occurring at the end of a year passed one third in a revival and one third in illustrations of the spirit of that revival in public discussions of topics of importance to New Lynn and New England, are invaluable as indications that you purpose that your church shall resist all the temptations incident to a crowded population. You mean that in no sense shall it be put on its knees to Labor on the one hand, or to Capital on the other, or to City Vices in any form; but on its knees only to Christ. "Scratch a Russian," said Napoleon, "and you will find beneath the surface a Tartar." Scratch an inefficient city church, and you will find beneath the surface a club. You mean that yours shall be a church, and not a club. You mean that it shall be as careful of Orthodoxy in Practice as of Orthodoxy in Doctrine. You mean that it shall not be unmindful of the teaching and the trials it has had in a long and not undistinguished past. Certain most serious and persistent misrepresentations of the history of the church for the last four months will be set at rest by these gifts. They are priceless to me for their own sakes, for the sake of these principles, and for your sakes. You have given me a picture of which the name is, The Sealers Crushed by the Icebergs. The true name of the picture of the winter, as you will allow me to say reverently, for the sake of New Lynn and New England, is, The Icebergs Crushed by the Sealers.(Applause.)

3

The Responses to the Lectures

INTRODUCTION TO THE COUNTER–LECTURE SERIES

The manufacturers, who were concerned about the negative image that Cook was presenting of the factory system, organized a counter–lecture series. The main lecture was delivered by a prominent manufacturer and President of the Board of Trade, George Keene. Keene's picture of the factory system stressed the community of interest and harmony between workers and manufacturers and also the importance of upward mobility as a reward for hard work. Keene minimized the impact of the mixing of sexes in the factory as an issue of morals and argued that the factories were a place for improvement, not degeneracy. Following Keene's talk several others in the community rose from the audience and challenged his view of the situation in Lynn.

The Reverend Mr. Cook then took the opportunity to disagree with Mr. Keene, and moreover to place himself on the side of the embattled workers and silent members of the community who wanted to speak out against the factory system but dared not for fear of retaliation. His response, although not going into any new area of conflict, guaranteed that the conflict stirred up in Lynn by the first three lectures would continue to keep the town alive with controversy.

THE COUNTER–LECTURE SERIES

The Manufacturers View, an Address by George Keene, Manufacturer and President of the Board of Trade

One week ago to-day the managers of this association very kindly and cordially invited me to make the opening debate this evening. I hesitated as to which subject would be the most useful to the cause of labor, and also the most suggestive for good. After deliberation it occurred to me that the "recent events," so-called, if taken up candidly from another stand-point, and if conducted free from personalities, would perhaps be the most productive of useful knowledge. I concluded to take that subject from the stand-point of a citizen and tax-payer interested in all the affairs of our city. With this explanation I will present you my views.

The consideration of the various statements recently made concerning the system adopted by the manufacturers of Lynn, and the liability of the present system tending to the moral degradation of the operators, has led me to examine somewhat into the facts, and review the situation of affairs in relation thereto. I do not assume to speak for any one but myself, and will present only my own observations, without the least unkindness to any person or persons who have been brought thus prominently before the public.

Assuming as a fair and honorable starting-point, and judging from what has been said and written, any fairminded and intelligent person would come to the conclusion that the system of manufacturing shoes, as at present adopted in our city, was, in a moral point of view, *needlessly and recklessly bad*; and the manufacturers themselves, if not directly implicated in the matter, were regardless of its consequences. This view I think any stranger, knowing nothing of our people, would be likely to take from reading or hearing the public statements that have been made. While I do not intend to say that Lynn or its system of labor is perfect, or its inhabitants free from the temptations and vices incident to human nature, I do intend to say that—although we have been called upon to introduce an entire change in our mode of manufacturing, in a very short space of time, which has brought into our midst a great addition to our population, both male and female — we are, on the whole, and on the average, as clear in the particular matters charged as any of our neighboring manufacturing towns and cities. Yea, more. I think Lynn will stand, when fairly weighed in the scale of absolute truth, fully up to the standard of the best manufacturing city you may select, in point of morality and good citizenship. But even then there is enough to do to keep busy every benevolent and moral enterprise that can be started. There are liabilities to temptation on our right and on our left, and no benevolent and Christian person, desirous of doing good among us, will find himself long out of work.

Situation of Affairs in Lynn. I have been intimately connected with the shoemaking business in Lynn, as workman and manufacturer, since

1826. I have watched carefully and interestedly the course of events through all the changes since that time, and have lived in Lynn over a half century. It is not wise for us or prudent for the community to cover up or to exaggerate difficulties or defects that may appear in the situation or the moral status of any business in the city or State; but it should be examined fairly, in the light of common sense, with an honest purpose to apply, if found defective, such remedies as an enlightened Christian community shall sanction and commend. Every citizen must know that our city, from its connection with the manufacure of shoes, has become an important place, both in population and the value of its productions. They must also know that it differs in one particular from other manufacturing places; that its wealth and business is in the hands of individual enterprise, and not in large factory corporations. Our prosperous manufacturers are men from the common walks of life, who, after toiling and struggling with the vicissitudes of business, are themselves the controlling power, and personally interested in our success.

Separation of the Sexes. It would not be surprising if some defects should appear in a system so suddenly introduced as the present mode of manufacturing shoes among us; for within the memory of most of us there were no females employed in our manufactories or in the shops of the workmen. The females found employment in their homes, binding and fitting the shoes, while the men made and prepared them. *Now* there are from three to five thousand women employed in the various factories in this city, in almost every department of industry connected with the business. They are found not only useful and efficient, but generally faithful and trustworthy. Shall we in this state of facts make the public statement, that the system is bad, because working in shops with men, the women and the youth of our city will be degraded and given to immorality? Is this true? Do we find our public schools productive of immorality because the boys and girls go to the same schools? Do we find the family less pure and liable to corruption because composed of boys and girls together? Is it not the experience of all mankind, that what is true of the nature of boys and girls continues with us through life very much after the same order? Jean Paul Richter says: "To insure modesty I would advise the education of the sexes together, for two boys will preserve twelve girls, or two girls twelve boys, *innocent,* amid winks, jokes and improprieties, merely by that instinctive sense, which is the forerunner of matured modesty. But I will guarantee nothing in a school where girls are alone together—still less where boys are alone." Do we find industry and labor productive of immoral conduct—or is it idleness and listlessness? I do not pretend to decide the exact fact, which is best—a separation of the sexes in the workshops or not; but this I think I can decide, that the chances for the result in the case of the five thousand women in our factories, engaged from morning till night each day in good, useful employment, or the selection of five thousand women out of any city in the country of equal population, without employment—however carefully they may be brought up—would be in favor of these Lynn shop girls making the best wives and mothers, and becoming the most useful citizens. Immoral conduct is not the peculiarity of Lynn, or in any manner the result of our system of business. It is as prolific in country villages, and every town and city, wherever it shall find nourishment in the hearts of people. In those places where woman is held by man in the lowest esteem it is most destructive and degrading, and in those places where woman is elevated to the true dignity and majesty of her womanhood, there we find the purest morality and the highest virtue.

It is the solemn duty of all honest citizens to discountenance and discourage immorality, or the appearance of it, in society. But in the fair and honorable discussion of the subject, we should never forget the great primal law of our being, that we cannot separate man from his humanity; for in all movements of society we see the liabilities and prerogatives of human nature go to make up the larger proportion of events in human progression, and are always on the whole, onward and upward. What society most needs in the progress of human concerns is *faith* in human nature. It is not all bad, nor all vicious; and what every man and woman needs to sustain him or her through great trials and great temptations is faith that the community *believe in them*; and if you would render them more liable to fall into the abyss of shameful temptations, teach them to feel that the community doubt them.

Effect of Careless Expressions. This, to my mind, is the desolating influence forced upon the public mind by the recent public discussion begun at Music Hall; it is a kind of an education which sermons and catechisms will scarcely undo. I think I can say, in justice, that every conscientious man in this community feels himself in some degree personally responsible for the public virtue; and from this cause comes the present conflict. Poisonous prejudices against classes are often instilled into the public mind by careless preaching or thoughtless expressions. For instance, let a person high in authority teach the people in Lynn that every person who makes a bad shoe loses the fire of his eye, and you will find every boy in the street looking into the eyes of his neighbor, and in time, if all his discoveries should be true, every workman would make bad shoes, and every eye lose its fire. And any statement of a similar nature, affecting the moral character of a class, is more disatrous to a community than even this.

Moral Aspect of the Question. The girls employed in our factories are largely composed of Americans, and mostly from good, honest, Christian families. Is it fair or honorable, in any true sense, to hurl the imputation broadcast that these shopwomen are immoral, and it would be dangerous to the morals of the young men to be in their company? Such a statement, repeated by an important member of our community, inflicts a wound upon society that will paralyze the efforts of the good in their kindly office of reform. Is it not rather the duty of every Christian minister, as well as every good citizen, to look fairly and honestly back to the cause? Every intelligent person ought to know that the human passions are the *most* important, yet the severest and most trying prerogatives belonging unto the race of man, and their correct discipline will make them the most exalted and noble principle that can render man honored and beloved of his race, and the beloved and honored in heaven. Too long, too long already, has this noble, God-given quality in human nature been wallowing in the mud and filth of stupid ignorance, writhing and struggling against ages of prejudice, hypocrisy, and sin, striving through all this shame and filth to make itself known and respected among men; for, when understood, it will be the greatest and highest principle that can produce peace, joy, and happiness. It is vested in our nature by our Creator for wise, holy, and exalted purposes. The violations of its high principles will surely return to us and our descendants in unmitigated sorrow. This truth is so solemn that no good citizen should ever dare refuse to utter or consider it; and I beg of you to remember that, while human passion is one of the elements which God has generously and liberally endowed us with, he has also given to us kingly and queenly authority over ourselves. To demoralize this high prerogative is to invite into our own *soul* a host of traitorous enemies, to destroy *all* that is beautiful and lovely within us. 'Tis the *idle* thought that corrupts us. 'Tis the *mind demoralized* that *lures* us into *error, vice,* and *sin.* 'Tis from within cometh the evil.

Call to mind that great and sublime truth uttered by Jesus, when he says: "He that *looketh* on a woman, to lust after her, hath committed adultery already in his heart." Can any person properly comprehend the tremendous meaning of these words, without considering the great amount of light and easy talk, the slanderous jesting about the virtue of the people, and the repeating of impure stories so habitually and carelessly, among all classes—rich and poor, upper and lower, white and black, male and female? Then ask ourselves if this is not cultivating and inviting lust, with all its issues, directly into the heart. To pick out the frailties and liabilities of poor human nature, and hold them up to contempt and ridicule, may be an easy task; but is it not catering to the lowest and meanest desires of the human soul? If we wish to do this, we shall find every human being in the universe frail enough for our purpose. We are all, every one, full of faults and imperfections, constantly stumbling, and constantly pleading at the Throne of Mercy for pardon. We know, also, that slanderous expressions and backbitings have a wonderfully prolific growth, which, if encouraged in any community, will sadly undermine, if not destroy, the efforts of the best, the truest, and purest laborers we have. *It is the very citadel of Satan*, his strongest breastwork and fortification, *the* battery from which his heaviest guns are discharged.

Without calling in question the motives of any one, I must give it as my solemn conviction, that the personal allusions that have been made, and which have found expression in our public journals—whether denied or contested in point of fact, or not,—have caused a large increase of public scandal, greatly to the detriment of public morals. Moreover, the high position from whence it emanated has fixed in the minds of the people in our neighboring towns and cities a most foul aspersion against the moral character of our young and prosperous city, which it will take years of our best efforts to undo. And the worst of all is, it has sent into the midst of this community a whole series of scandals, giving rich food to nourish all the vile contemplations of sensuality, wherein dwelleth all the seeds of lust.

Undue Alarm as to Female Employment. With this preface, I will give to you what I believe to be the condition of the present system of our manufactories, and the reason for the employment of female labor. Not that it is necessary for the defense of Lynn or her people, in respect to their morals or habits and customs, but because very erroneous opinions may be formed by very honest people in our own midst, as to the true situation of affairs among us; and because, if silent, it might be inferred, by equally honest people, that the whole budget of statements *were true*, and could not be fairly answered. With all kindly feeling and honorable regard for every good intention and true purpose of reform attempted to be instituted in the recent discussion concerning the morals of these workpeople, it does appear to me that they must have been misinformed, or, through alarm, must have misapprehended the facts in the case. The manufacturers of Lynn are certainly not the men to shrink from any moral responsibility that may publicly rest upon them, and, had they been consulted by any one with sincere desire of doing good to their workpeople, would have found efficient aid in this most useful field of labor. I venture to assert that there is not a manufacturer among us who, if his attention was properly called to any defect, either in his building or his arrangements of labor, but would gladly avail himself of the hint, and, if in his judgment correct, would adopt it.

Shoemakers Generally Well Educated. The Lynn shoemakers—or, more properly, those brought up under the old system—are, generally speaking, very well and properly informed upon all subjects, both in national and state affairs, in private and public matters, and are not behind any other class in intelligence or understanding of the general observations of facts and fancies, and are not often known to be afraid to look facts squarely in the face. They have their own opinions upon all subjects, and are not afraid to utter them; and this is the class and style of men now controlling Lynn. The independence of the nature of their business encourages this liberal feeling in our midst. The first year the town of Lynn assumed to make an estimate of the valuation of her property was in 1830, when her whole taxable wealth was found to be a little rising $1,800,000! Our schoolhouses were small and inadequate, our churches poor and far between, and the dwellings of the people and shops of the manufacturers and workmen corresponded with the churches and schoolhouses. Let any intelligent citizen or stranger look over our city to-day, and he will tell you that in point of the arrangements of our streets, the convenient style and extent of our schools, the beauty of our private residences, the elegance of our churches and City Hall, the stability and convenience of our manufactories, they are equal to those in any of the manufacturing towns or cities in the state.

No Wealth from Other Cities. And all this has not come to us of itself; it has been accomplished by the intense labor and earnest efforts of our own citizens. We had no foreign help, no wealthy neighbors to pour into our laps their overflowing wealth. We had no inducements to offer them. We were only the makers of and dealers in shoes; and in earlier days this was considered not a very promising or fashionable business. Not only have this generation improved and adorned their own city, but, by upright and judicious conduct, have largely contributed to render the business of shoemaking not only honorable and respectable, but one of the most important branches of industry in the country. In the progress of this growth I could relate to you numerous incidents of thrilling interest connected with nearly every manufacturer in Lynn. One only will I relate, as it illustrates the character of our people. During the continuance of the World's Industrial Fair, at the Crystal

Palace in New York, one of the Queen's Commissioners from England visited Lynn, in order to inform himself and his government how the workmen were managed in the shoemaking districts of this country. He was introduced to one of our manufacturers, and, after a strict examination into our mode of doing business, he expressed himself much surprised that we should trust our workmen with so much material to work up, without a stamp put upon the pieces by which to know them. Just at that moment one of his workmen came in with some work, and the manufacturer introduced him to the Commissioner, when an animated discussion arose between them upon subjects of state and national politics, religion, and trade. The Commissioner turned to the manufacturer, and said: "I don't wonder you trust your workmen, if this is a specimen, for he has beaten me on every tack."

Employment of Female Laborers. The first attempt to introduce women's labor, to any extent, into our factories, was on the introduction of the sewing-machine, about the time of the adoption of our city form of government. Then the question of the moral propriety was fully considered and freely discussed by the manufacturers. Then our conveniences were unfavorable: there were no factories of sufficient size to properly accommodate them. Yet the attempt proved a success; and I think the universal experience of every manufacturer who thus early introduced the sewing-machines is, that the girls created a favorable influence in the factory. They earned better pay, and were more independent in their labors. And the moral result is practically this— that these girls thus early called together have become, in most cases, worthy members of society, and are now honored as wives and mothers among us. This I know to be the case in reference to the girls in two of three of the earlier manufactories. Since then, in the construction of every building for the purpose of manufacturing, every attention has been paid to the convenience and comfort of these operatives. The machines have been greatly improved, and also the mode of operating them so as to give more ease, as well as to guard the health of the laborer. Of course, there are many factories that are not large, yet still employ girls; but as fast as these manufacturers can enlarge their premises they do so, and always introduce the proper conveniences. The largest portion of the girls employed in Lynn are now employed in these departments, and I believe it to be the expressed opinion of a majority of all the manufacturers that they are orderly and well-behaved, and entirely free from the loose and vicious conduct imputed to them. Every day their shops are visited by strangers, coming in at different times, and they are always found busily engaged, decorous, respectful, and orderly; and whoever visited the fair of the Grand Army, held at Music Hall last week, must have been profoundly impressed on seeing that great crowd of both men and women, each day and evening during the week, intermixed and intermingling throughout the entire building, consisting of thousands of our fellow-citizens of both sexes, and not a word, a look, or action observable by any one that could detract from the lady or the gentleman; and the ladies in these gatherings were largely composed of our Lynn shop-girls.

With the introduction of the McKay sewing-machine, a great change has been made in the mode of manufacturing shoes, by a systematic division of labor. With the favorable experience had in the employment of female help thus far, the manufacturer believed that many parts could be as well performed by women as by men; and wherever the circumstances are favorable, they invariably improve the condition of things around them. This system of making shoes has greatly consolidated our labor. Women are employed wherever their labor can be available, and in a large majority of factories, where they are at work with men, better order and decorum is manifest. The most important necessity felt by the manufacturer has been hitherto, is now, and always will be, the employment of the right person as superintendent. Experience only can prove what is the best mode of action in this comparatively new system of business. It would be the most disastrous thing that could befall the progress of woman's labor in our city, to have our manufacturers lose their faith in them. It is, therefore, the duty of every good citizen to do all in his power to elevate the true character of woman.

Business of Lynn Self-Made. There is really less want of harmony between the employer and employed in Lynn than in any other place I am acquainted with, and there is really more kindly sympathy between the manufacturer and his workmen in our business than is usual in any other business. It is in the nature of business to bring manufacturer and workmen into harmony, because their interests are identical. There is in Lynn no aristocracy of wealth, or family. The leading men of Lynn show prominently to the world that with us the poor of to-day will be the rich of to-morrow. This harmony of interest in Lynn is manifested by the meetings and friendly consultations of both parties last year, and the adoption of plans and arrangements mutually beneficial. There may be differences of opinion among us, but you will rarely find a business of so much importance as ours where the manufacturer feels that true interest in his workmen, and the workmen an equal interest in the success of the manufacturer; and the result has been (I am proud to say it) that Lynn today stands in the front rank with all the best cities in the Union, in point of business integrity and standing. And why should she not also in morality?

It is undoubtedly true that there is liability to an increase of moral impurity in all mixed communities, where the people know but little of each other. But every laborer, even in that field of reform, to be useful, must be patient, and by *wisdom* learn how to direct his efforts so as to benefit and improve that condition, rather than by haste to injure it. The efforts of the Woman's Mission for Christian Work, with many other associations among us, are silently doing noble work in this direction. Let any citizen go into our public schools, and there behold the thousands of bright and happy children gathered from every family in Lynn, see the good order, decorum and discipline, and reflect how cheerfully the public treasure is poured out like water, to nourish and support them. And that treasure is furnished largely from the factory operations in our midst. Then ask yourself if the larger proportion of these beautiful children will not necessarily take their places side by side with the industry of this city, and become the operatives in these factories. Then what party is there in Lynn so cruel or thoughtless as to fasten the stigma of impurity upon these factories, which are and must be the hope of the city—the stay of the people—our only source of wealth? Rather let every citizen go forth clad in the rough habiliments of labor, ready to do every true and honest work in the cause of our children, in the cause of our city, and the cause of virtue and of God.

A High School Principal's Response to Keene's Address

The following is a synopsis of the remarks of the different speakers who followed Mr. Keene at the Labor Reform Meeting, on Thursday evening last, which, owing to the crowded state of our columns, were omitted in our report of Saturday.

Mr. Henry Moore, principal of the Franklin-street grammar school, said that in the discussion of this question of Labor Reform—in fact, in the discussion of any question—*truth*, and not victory, or an unjust interest, ought to be the object; and keeping this in view, he did not see any occasion for anybody to get angry or excited. He thought it best to discuss this whole matter calmly and dispassionately. Many of the statements and arguments of the lecturer he should not dissent from, but he thought he had misapprehended the position of the gentleman who spoke in Music Hall. It was a very *easy* but not a very *just* mode of argument, to place our antagonist in a *false* position and then batter down the false position. Such arguments might be very good for some purposes, but they utterly failed to touch the *real* position of our opponent. He did not think it just to accuse the gentleman who spoke in Music Hall of intentionally slandering Lynn, when he *opened* the discussion of this question with remarks *highly complimentary* to the enterprise, intelligence, and general good order and morality of the people in this city. There are moral evils and perils connected with the manufacturing system of Lynn, which every candid and intelligent person who has given the matter any thought, must admit. These evils may not be greater than exist in other large manufacturing centres, but yet they do exist, and what harm will come if we look these evils fairly in the face as honest men and Christians. The man who advocates sanitary provisions for a city is not generally considered an enemy to the health and prosperity of that city. Mr. Moore thought the lecturer was unfortunate in his comparison of the mixing of the sexes in the shoe factories with the relation of boys and girls in our schools. For every one knows that the teacher is always present, that no talking is allowed, and in many schools not even whispering. For his part, he could not see any analogy in the two cases. He thought the lecturer had said some good things, but he had not touched the real positions of the gentleman who spoke at Music Hall.

Workers Respond to Keene

Mr. Samuel A. Bancroft said that he agreed with the remarks of Mr. Moore. He said that he had worked in the shops of Lynn for twenty years, and he knew what he was talking about when he said that Mr. Cook had not told half the truth about the evils in these shops. He had followed the sea, and had travelled the country considerably in his lifetime, but he had never heard such vile and filthy language as he had heard uttered in the shoe shops of Lynn. If gentlemen wanted facts, he could find facts. What had been said at Music Hall concerning the manufactories was true. He had heard, in Mr. Keene's own factory, language the foulest that could come from a man's mouth. He said there was no use in trying to cover these things up, or to deny them, for everybody who knows anything about the matter knows that they do exist.

Mr. Samuel Porter said, that as he understood it to be in order to discuss this or former lectures, he wished to say a few words in opposition to one of the positions taken in a former lecture, in regard to the Crispins. The lecturer did not say Crispins, but he knew he meant them, when he talked about some of their positions not being democratic, about their having rotten timber in their vessel, which, if not removed, would sink it. Mr. Porter said that he would cite three illustrations to prove that their position was democratic. The illustrations cited were the tarriff, life-insurance, and the church.

Mr. Thomas Roberts said that he thought it was a very poor plan for people to get angry every time anyone said anything which did not harmonize with their views. If, in the course of his remarks he should say anything which did not harmonize with the views of any one present, he hoped that they would not get angry about it. He said that he did not believe in the Crispin organization. He was opposed to a monopoly of muscle, just as much as to a monopoly of money. He opposed it, because he thought that in the end it would injure the working class more than any one else. He had contended that the strike of 1860 injured the working class, and benefited the manufacturer by enabling him to clean out all his old stock of goods. He said that he heard Mr. Cook's lecture in Music Hall, and he thought that he was talking for the best good of the laboring class, and they pretty generally so understood it.

Mr. Charles J. Butler remarked that a good deal had been said in these discussions about being born in Lynn. He had not that to boast of; but he trusted he was just as good a citizen nevertheless, and had the interest of the city as much at heart as any other resident. He had imbibed some pretty strong American ideas, and cited an incident to prove it which occurred during a recent visit "across the water." In company with several gentlemen they met another, whose outward form was the same as their own, but to whom his companions tipped their hats, in token of obeisance. Upon inquiry, he learned that it was Lord somebody, and that it was customary in that country to salute the gentry in the manner related; but, he said, he cherished too strong American sentiments to tip his hat to even a lord, or to any one else, on account of his wealth. He afterwards, learned, too, that this lord was an oppressor of the poor, as was oftentimes the case. Mr. Butler said he did not believe in looking up to any man as superior, *merely* because he possesses wealth. He thought it important that the capitalist and laborer should understand each other better; and one important point to be ascertained in these discussions, when evils are found to exist, is, *how* to apply the remedy. He believed that, throughout the city, in nineteen out of twenty workrooms, both males and females would vote for a separation of the sexes; and the passage of Scripture referred to by the speaker this evening (Matt. v. 28) is one of the strongest arguments why they should be separated. This being so, let the females be placed by themselves, and thereby remove the temptation.

Cook's Reply to Mr. Keene's Address

In regard to the opening address delivered at the recent Labor meeting in this city, it is hardly necessary that I should say anything after the five speeches which were immediately volunteered in reply to it.

(1) The address is courteous. I rejoice to recognize its courtesy.

(2) It does not take ground decisively against the separation of the sexes. It says: "I do not pretend to decide the exact fact, which is best, a separation of the sexes in the workshops, or not."

If I say a frank word or so as to the argument of the address, I must not be understood as personal, for I am speaking of the argument, and not of its author.

1. As an argument, the address is up to its knees in what I call the high-school swamp. (Applause.) Five circumstances distinguish the relations of sexes mingled in a high school from those relations in the workroom of a factory. (2) The immoral are excluded from the high school. (2) The sexes there mingled have homes of their own and the restraint of social ties close at hand. (3) Usually they are persons of refined tastes, or whose most important object is to acquire those tastes. (4) They are constantly under the eye of a teacher. (5) Religious exercises open or close the school. Now, when this address, written by President of the Board of Trade, claims that the present arrangements of the factory system here have been carefully studied, and then gives as a specimen of that carefulness the overlooking of distinctions as wide and clear as these; and says that, because Jean Paul Frederick Richter— I have a high respect for Richter's authority—remarks that the sexes ought to be educated together, the inference is that they should work together in rooms filled at hap-hazard from a floating population through a door that is not a sieve, it is not too much to say that the address is up to its knees in the high-school swamp. A not graceful position for the genial President of the Board of Trade!

2. The address is self-contradictory in its claims. It asserts and insinuates that Lynn, in respect to "all the matters charged," is equal to any manufacturing town in New England. It then puts forward the plea that the system here is very young, and that its imperfections must be excused on that ground. These two claims cannot be made in the same breath. It would be singular indeed if the shoe factory system,

which has begun within ten years, were already as perfect as the cotton factory system, which has been carefully studied for two hundred. The "matters charged" are that the shoe factory system here exhibit carelessness on important points. That the system of Lynn is young is the one strong point of excuse for it. But it is getting late to call it young. Property that will not change its shape for fifty years is being invested in it here every day.

3. It is claimed in this address that as fast as the great firms here are able they make "all proper" arrangements for their operatives. I simply deny this. Many of the great firms do. But the poet Tennyson praises Prince Albert for devoting his time to studying the models of lodging-houses. The most delicate-minded of the English poets praises the noblest of the recent English princes for studying the arrangements for cottage workrooms, kitchens, and even sewers. Would that some Prince Albert and Poet Tennyson might criticise certain very wealthy firms here, who have incomes of a hundred thousand a year, and yet make only the most wretched and inadequate provisions on points Prince Albert did not disdain to study.

4. The address fails to meet the decisive points of the case. I do not call the argument evasive, for I believe it honest as well as courteous. It fails to meet the points that the advertising board, through which operatives are engaged, is not a sieve; that the percentage of changeable operatives is high; that the floating population of a shoe town is likely to be large; that foul mouths in factories are well understood to be part of the problem; that physicians of this city solemnly testify that important evils result from the present arrangements; and that corporation boarding-houses cannot be in a shoe town what they are in a cotton town.

When the hunter on the Amazon sees a certain shadow on the ground at midday, he knows that the Amazonian vulture hangs above in the air. I have not seen the vulture. I am much mistaken if I have not seen his shadow. Working men have said to me that they do not dare discuss this subject for fear their wages will be reduced. I was told by one of the best representatives of their interests that they feared to agitate this theme because of apprehension that the Board of Arbitration or Conference, between employers and employed, so sensibly organized here, might be disturbed in its operations. A gentleman of the highest intelligence and culture told me he prepared two articles for the press, in support of the improvements suggested, and one of them he read to me; but keeping in mind the treatment of certain parties in the past, he decided not to publish the articles, and was advised by his friends not to publish; for fear of unscrupulous attack by petty business annoyances from rich men. A most intelligent lady told me that she had prepared an article in support of the interests of the working class in this discussion, and was induced by her husband not to print it, solely because of the fear of unscrupulous attack by petty business annoyances. I have in mind a score of unimpeachable illustrations. More than twenty times, and I think more than fifty, I have crossed this shadow; and more than six times I have crossed it within my own parish. The fear of attack from rich men! This I call the shadow of the Amazonian vulture. I hope it is only a cloud of exaggeration which casts it. But when one sees the shadow twenty or fifty times, that is enough to found an inference on, stout enough to cause a man at least to look up. (Applause.)—*Lynn Semi-Weekly Reporter*, March 15, 1871; *Lynn Transcript*, March 18, 1871.

OTHER CONTEMPORARY DOCUMENTS

Manufacturers' Responses to Cook's Lectures

Mr. Cook and His Statements

MR. EDITOR: We desire, in as few words as practicable, and in behalf of the girls in our employ who were so falsely slandered by Mr. Cook, in the lecture recently delivered by him in Music Hall, to call upon Mr. Cook for an apology. Waiving all information which he claims to have received, we call him to an account for what he said in regard to the girls based upon his own judgment. Mr. Cook said in his lectures, in speaking of the shop, that when he entered, he picked out the girl who had resisted temptation; but that *all* the others were bad—so bad that no virtuous young man could remain in the room with them any length of time and remain virtuous.

Looking at the audience, he asked them how they supposed he was enabled to select the virtuous girl from the bad. He answered the question by remarking that after a woman had fallen, there were certain unmistakable signs by which the fall could be detected; that they had lost the flash and lustre of the eye, the bloom and rosy hue of the cheek, and in their place the haggard look is seen; and that was the condition of those he saw in this room, and that was how he knew.

Now, without having any desire to call in question Mr. Cook's vast experience in that particular direction, or that he may be eminently qualified to read the human face, still we think he must admit that in this instance his judgment was not infallible, and in consequence of his remarks being unqualifiedly false, and by their having been made, an act of great injustice was done, we call on him, as an act of simple justice on his part, to make a full and complete retraction of the remarks, in as public a manner as said remarks were made.

BERRY AND BEEDE

Lynn Semi-Weekly Reporter, February 15, 1871.

The License of the Pulpit

MR. EDITOR: The late Doctor Cooke, whose name and fame will be ever held in reverence by every true citizen of Lynn, has left on record this quaint comment, not altogether complimentary, perhaps, but nevertheless believed by him to be true, that, "if Satan has any degrading and filthy delusion to play off, to bring the human race into greater contempt, Lynn is the place which he wont to choose for its birth." Had the great and good man foreseen that his own pulpit was destined to serve as the special birthplace, he would not so willingly have laid aside the armor in which he had so long and faithfully served; yet it seems to have been reserved for his direct successor to prove that the satire was not altogether undeserved, and that the occasion for it did not die with the genial critic who originated it.

Our community has been considerably excited, of late, and certainly not without good cause, by certain wholesale accusations publicly made by the present Rev. Mr. Cook, from what he regarded for the time as his own pulpit; and, although certain mild communications, both in support and in attempted mitigation of the offence, have from time to time appeared, it seems to me that the press of our city has hardly kept pace with public sentiment in the matter; remaining silent, doubtless, from a delicacy commendable in itself, and hoping that, through silence and neglect, the affair would die a natural death. But such a fate, however desirable, seems hardly possible in this case. The slander has found ready ears outside, and the rival manufacturing cities are only too glad to believe and spread the report. The press of these cities has repeated and commented upon it; and if, as we claim, the slander is baseless and false, they have a right to expect its refutation here, where it originated. Our manufacturers are daily in receipt of letters from their correspondents, really of regret and condolence over the depraved state of our society, taking the truth of it for granted, as either admitted or proved. Our former fellow-citizens, now located elsewhere, write to their friends in sorrow that their native city has so degenerated, and lament the change in our business that has brought with it the seemingly inevitable attendants, vice and immorality.

From all this, it is painfully evident that the fair fame of our city has suffered, and not inconsiderably, from this wanton attack upon the character of its citizens; and yet the reverend calumniator, though earnestly appealed to, wraps himself in his clerical dignity, and doggedly refuses "to bate a single word or take a letter back." Far be it from me to detract from the dignity and sanctity which New England education or prejudice has thrown around the sacred desk and the office of which it is the type and symbol; yet we deem it no heresy to regard those filling it as men of flesh and blood like ourselves, and with like passions, prejudices, and responsibilities too; and a slander, public or private, can claim no immunity from the laws of honor or of society because it issues from the pulpit.

As to the nature of the offence, as we choose to call it, of the reverend gentleman, no comment is needed, for it is already too well known to all of us; but a word as to the defence offered by his friends, since he himself does not condescend to unbend himself, either in defence or explanation, and which appears to be simply this that, so far as the slander was fastened directly upon individuals, it was a private conversation and should not have been divulged; or, in other words, that only the *public* virtue and *general* reputation of our city were *publicly* attacked; *private* character and reputation having been allowed the privilege of a private and confidential execution. How this helps the matter, or mitigates the offence, I fail to see. That conversation has been divulged, and was first made public by his own friends, and has since been published in full, and in the public mind is inseparably connected with, and a part of, the general slander; and, more than that, the author still maintains it as true, and we must take him at his word.

All that is, however, immaterial here, for it is with the public and general slander that we have particularly to do. And to that point we submit, that it is a fair and logical deduction from the reverend gentleman's discourse, that among the operatives in our city, disorder and licentiousness constitute the rule, and good order, virtue, and chastity, the exception. Certainly we find no outward manifestations of this lamentable state of things. We defy the reverend gentleman or his supporters and friends, to point to a city of the business and population of Lynn, where fewer offences against the law committed, or where good order is so distinctive a feature of all public occasions and places. A lady unattended can walk our streets, at any reasonable hour of the day or night, secure from harm or insult, and our police record will compare most favorably with that of any town or city in the Common-wealth. Such, we submit, is the character of our city, and we are each and all justly proud of it, and it certainly seems cruel and unjust that a reputation so fairly earned should be thus publicly assailed from individual caprice or ambition; and still worse, if the attack is the offspring of a diseased imagination, that it should receive moral support and character from the endorsement of the church, society, or community to which its author temporarily belongs.

It is not unreasonable to suppose that a person of ordinary prudence, before assailing the reputation of an individual or a community, would possess himself of facts or information in his justification. Yet here no facts are cited, and those whom the gentleman has quoted as his informants publicly deny their responsibility. But the reverend gentleman does not depend upon facts or proofs—a magical power of insights, vouchsafed to him alone, explains it all. He claims to possess a power of vision so wonderful that he can at will pierce the ordinarily impenetrable outside surface, and clearly discern secrets unrevealed to ordinary mortals. This power is intensified to infallibility at a certain season of the year, and, unfortunately for the victims, they were submitted to his scrutiny during "his month"—"The eye month," the weird month of January. We have been educated in the belief that "the secret things belong unto the Lord our God"; but that was written long ago, and this is New England and the nineteenth century, and here, in the midst of us, is His viceregent, with the divine attribute fully developed and in practical use, and each and all of us, with our wives and families, must pass at his option in review before this infallible judge, and be stamped and catalogued as to our fealty to virtue or vice in accordance with his decree. "Whence hath this man this wisdom, and these mighty works?" Where such a power exists, is it unreasonable that we should look for a commensurate responsibility; and have not the public whose honor is assailed, and the individuals whose characters are defamed, a right to demand where such responsibility rests? If the author of the calumny is irresponsible, as we in charity believe, where else shall we look save to those who have publicly endorsed his course, and so given in its only claim even to public condemnation? His church has already done so officially, and so have many of his over-zealous friends. Surely such zeal must be encouraging to a pastor, and is certainly commendable so long as the pastor is right; but it is simply intolerant bigotry when he is wrong.

Meanwhile, outraged public sentiment righteously demands of that pastor, and those of his people who uphold him, that they justify the slander by its proof, or retract it as publicly as it was uttered. LYNN. *Lynn Semi-Weekly Reporter,* March 4, 1871.

A Factory Owner's Letter

MR. EDITOR: I learn that Flavius Josephus Cook is about to close his career in Lynn. I have waited to the utmost limit of time for an apology from him in relation to the unjust attack in which he slanderously maligned and injured those unprotected and innocent women who work in a factory which belongs to me—hoping that common decency would prompt him to repair an injury that he had done, so far as was in his power. He doggedly and persistently refuses to do so. The language he uses relative to them is so vile and obscene that I cannot repeat it, and could emanate only from a heart wicked and malicious. And if he leaves town with this hanging over him—when they have kindly offered to forgive him, if he will only make a square apology—it should follow him wherever he goes.

I learn that he talks of leaving our shores for Germany, because, having graduated from several seminaries here, and got all the learning that our country affords, he can learn nothing more here. Now, Flavius Josephus, I think there many things more you can learn in this country. I think you could learn to be modest, and possibly might learn to be gentlemanly, should you make it your study. Learn to be pure in thought and word; learn to be agreeable in manner; learn to honor and respect woman. It betrays a defect in early education to speak disrespectfully of women, and the kindly affection one should cherish towards his mother would seem to forbid it. You have repeatedly said that you felt like Bismark before Paris, and last that you felt like Bismark *in* Paris, exulting in victory. The only victory you have gained is over these innocent and unprotected women. To exult in that bespeaks a spirit not of heaven or of earth. The rest of your career has been one complete defeat. You have ill-treated your own people, and insulted every one who dared to differ from you. I hope you leave Lynn a wiser if not a better man.

S. M. BUBIER

Lynn Semi-Weekly Reporter, May 6, 1871.

COMMUNITY RESPONSES TO COOK'S LECTURES

The Reverend Joseph Cook's depiction of the immoral conditions in the factories and the immoral characters of the operatives created a great stir in the city of Lynn. Many in the audience began to speculate about the identity of the factory to which Cook referred. The result of that speculation, and the public reporting of a private conversation between Cook and a small group of civic leaders, led to the identification of one particular factory in the public mind. The owners and employees of the factory suspected of being a den of immorality were indirectly accused of immorality. In response, they denounced Cook. In Lecture III, Cook addressed his attackers and claimed that he did not refer to a specific factory and that, moreover, the community supported him in his attack on the immorality of the present factory system. After this lecture Mr. S. M. Bubier, a manufacturer, rose to the stage and demanded to speak out to refute Cook's accusations. Many in the audience prepared to leave but Cook, playing upon the occasion, urged them to stay.

Bubier stated he knew of no factory which fit the description of Cook's immoral system. Bubier also claimed that, having lived and done business in the city, for some fifty-five years, he was more knowledgeable of conditions in the factory than Cook, who had been in the city only seven months. Bubier then made a reference to Cook's residence in the McLean Asylum, at which point the audience forced him to leave the stage with hissing and booing.

Response to the lectures was not confined to applause, hissing, or even Mr. Bubier's public rejoinder. The local papers were also filled with letters about the lectures. Some of the letters, particularly from the middle class, supported Cook. Members of the Society of the First Congregational Church met in a special meeting and endorsed Cook's views. Mrs. Glover, whose husband was a skilled carpenter, added her support for Cook's attacks against "crimes in community least rebuked." As the wife of a skilled carpenter, Mrs. Glover saw herself in a world separate from both the manufacturers and the workers, particularly the unskilled immigrants. Her perspective was that of the older Protestant artisans, who identified with neither the new working class nor the manufacturers. Her hostility to the latter was apparent in her support for Cook, as was her lack of sympathy for those caught within the factory system. Her alternative was to call upon an older Christian community (which may have existed only in her nostalgic idealization of the past), which gave strength and meaning to those artisans who shared neither the values of the new manufacturers nor the world of the unskilled workers. "Purity is the baptism of scientific Christianity; it should be insisted upon. . . ." Mrs. Glover's position was supported and joined by many of the older workers of the city. Usually those workers who supported Cook emphasized the ideals of traditional artisan culture, independence, and antimonopoly. Identifying with neither the unskilled workers nor the manufacturers, they hoped to find an alternative to both these groups in Cook's moral community.

Not all workers found in Cook's message reason for support, Cook's portrayal of "the evils of the factory system" emphasized the "corrupting effects of the factory system on the workers." Cook had intended this focus to demonstrate his concern for the workers, a concern rooted in his sympathy for the poor. Yet those characterized as corrupt perceived this paternalistic concern to be a slur. They believed that they were singled out for this attack because they were forced to labor for survival. At the bottom of the economic ladder, the workers were subject not only to low wages and economic insecurity, but to paternalistic attacks on their character. They rejected Cook's characterization of them as "course, low, vulgar and bad featured," called attention to their identity as laborers, and accused Cook of attacking them for being working class. As the lectures proceeded, their position was taken up by the local Catholic priest, who saw the attacks as not only antiworking-class, but also anti-Catholic. An antagonistic position was also taken by the labor press, which interpreted Cook's comments as being antiworking-class. While not wanting to appear to oppose moral reform, the voice of Lynn's organized labor accused Cook of unfairly attacking the women who worked to support themselves, and called on the workers of the city to ignore Cook and remain united as a class.

Most of the comments included in this section of the book were either letters to the papers concerning the lectures or direct reporting in the local press. The first card reflects the feelings of the members of the First Congregational Church as to the success of the lectures, and reflects the image of Cook—which he was so careful to cultivate—as the embattled reformer taking on all comers. Others who responded to the lecture series were not as generous to either the Reverend Mr. Cook or his character.

A Card

At an informal meeting of the First Congregational Church and Society, convened at the close of divine service, Jan. 29th, the following resolution was unanimously adopted, and ordered to be printed in the several Lynn papers:

Whereas certain statements have been publicly made, in which the veracity of our acting pastor, Rev. Joseph Cook, has been called in question, and his standing with this Society as a Christian minister attacked; therefore,

RESOLVED, That this Society have the most entire confidence in the integrity, Christian character, and standing of our said pastor; and that we, as a Society, most heartily and cordially approve of his boldness, ability, and fidelity in presenting, both publicly and privately, those truths which, though unwelcome to some in this community, need to be plainly spoken in this day of increasing immorality and vice; and that our confidence in him as a Christian minister is unabated by the fearless manner with which he has withstood all attempts to intimidate and thwart him in his attempts thus publicly to perform an unpleasant but important Christian duty.

Per order,
FRANK P. BREED,
Parish Clerk,

Lynn, January 30, 1871.

A Card

I would hereby tender my sincere thanks to the Rev. Mr. Cook for the truly Christian stand he has taken as watchman on the walls of Zion to cry aloud and spare not those crimes in community least rebuked, and therefore the more fearful and devastating. Purity is the baptism of scientific Christianity; it should be insisted upon; and may his pulpit eloquence shatter the hoary fabric of ancient Sodom, and place mankind upon an eminence where the beams from the sun of truth first strike.

MRS. M. M. GLOVER

To the Public

Rev. Joseph Cook of Lynn, made a statement in Music Hall, during his last lecture, to this effect: That he visited a room in Lynn, from sixty to seventy feet in length, and some twenty feet in width, in which, at one end were six or eight girls employed as stitchers—at the other end were as many men. They were coarse, low, vulgar, bad-featured girls. A man who showed him the room informed him that no young man could come to that room a virtuous man and remain so any length of time, because the girls were so bad.

We the undersigned, believing we are the persons alluded to, feel that his charges are very unjust and unchristian, and we feel justified in appealing to an honest public to investigate our characters, and see whether the investigation will warrant any person in making such charges as these against those whom we believe have nothing to condemn them but that they are compelled to labor for their own maintenance.

[Names of eight female and of six male employees, omitted.]

To the Public

I understand that the Rev. Joseph Cook claims that he got the foregoing statements from me. In the first place I never made them. They are untrue if made by any one. It *is not* the character of this room. Nor do I know of any room of which the Rev. gentleman would be justified in making any such statement.

HENRY DOWNING

The Absorbing Topic

As we write, the all-absorbing topic in this city is the *denouement* at Music Hall last Sunday evening. The merits and demerits of the principals in that unhappy affair are freely discussed in parlors and workshops and on the streets. The unhealthy excitement caused by this affair had almost decided us to refrain from referring to the subject at all; and it is with feelings of great reluctance that we allude to it, and we only do so to satisfy the demands of an excited and expectant public. The unchristian feelings generated in society by this affair are greatly to be deplored; and however pure the motives of the principals in it may have been, the effect is unpleasant to contemplate. Although comparatively a stranger among us, the Rev. Mr. Cook has attracted much attention by his bold and fearless manner in presenting his sermons to the public; and even before we became acquainted with him we commended him for his frank, outspoken style, and for the interest which he appeared to take in the labor question and the general welfare of the masses. We were present at Music Hall, a week ago last Sunday night, and heard him make bold, astounding, and yet guarded, statements relative to the morals of those employed in the workshops of this city, in which remarks he cited the sources from which he had obtained his information, without, however, mentioning the names of persons. As has been alleged, he did then and there make certain broad and sweeping statements relative to the immoral condition of a workshop, which he described by an apparent guess at the length and breadth, and by an approximate estimate of the number of males and females employed therein, at the same time stating that personal observation coupled with the broad statements previously referred to, and which he claimed to be a quotation from the remarks of a male employee who conducted him through the establishment. Believing him to be honest in his motives, convictions, and statements, and knowing—as every observing citizen knows—that society, especially in large towns and cities, has been sadly demoralized since the breaking out of the rebellion, we were prepared to hear that our own city was not an exception to the general rule; but we frankly admit that, had not the statement about which there has been so much excitement been given as a quotation, we could not, in the absence of proofs, have done less than to attribute it to a misconception of facts or an overwrought imagination. In regard to the correctness of the other leading statements made by the speaker on the evening mentioned, we refer the public to the authorities which he cited. We left the hall that night with mingled feelings of sorrow for the sad condition of society, as portrayed by the speaker, and admiration for the man who, zealous for the cause which he has espoused, and apparently honest in his convictions and intentions, beards the lion in his den, fearless of the consequences. "To err is human; to forgive, divine." Mr. Cook, in his zeal, and by his bold, sharp, self-reliant, persevering, and determined attacks upon sin wherever found—making no distinctions between that clothed in broadcloth and fine linen and that habited in rags—has, as such men always have, aroused an opposition. There evidently has been a latent opposition to Mr. Cook ever since his advent among us.

There were, and still are, many here, as elsewhere, to whom the unveiled picture of sin in its naked hideousness strikes terror and dismay, and to them its exhibitor is an unwelcome visitor. On the Monday following the delivery of the sermon which has created such a sensation, the opposition to Mr. Cook began to assume outward form, increasing each day in certain quarters and in the course of three days his remarks had been so distorted and enlarged that the originals were unrecognizable. We are told that on Thursday he was interviewed, in his own parlor, by two prominent shoe manufacturers, one or both of whom had been led to believe that he (Mr. Cook) had referred to their shop in what was substantially claimed as an unwarrantable and morally offensive statement made by him in a public sermon on the Sunday evening previous. After being assured by Mr. Cook that he did not refer to either of their shops they desired him to name the place to which he did refer. In his own parlor, in private conversation, he frankly, but—as the sequel proved—injudiciously, located the room in question. If we are correctly informed the information obtained from Mr. Cook was immediately conveyed to the proprietors of the shop, and they, as well as their employees, and the two manufacturers previously mentioned, came out with a card to the public, denying the charges of immorality in the statement to which we have several times referred. That much indignation should be felt by those on whom the blow had fallen is not at all surprising, and it is peculiarly unfortunate for all concerned that the blow should have fallen where it is said it was least deserved. The moral status of the employees in the shop in question is reputed to be specially good, and it seems incredible that a man professing to preach the gospel should wantonly assail the characters of innocent females who earn their bread by daily toil, and this hinges the subject on a question of veracity between Mr. Cook and a male employee in the establishment, the latter flatly denying that he ever used the language quoted by the former and laid at his (the operative's) door. Although Mr. Cook gave the language—at which special offence has been taken—as a quotation, and confidently asserts that the male employee told it to him, yet in view of the fact—we have no doubt that it is a fact—that the moral condition of the shop mentioned will compare favorably with any in the city, we presume that Mr. Cook will make the *amende honorable* to the female employees of the establishment. Unless he can show that the statement made upon heresay—as he claims—is true, he owes an apology to the ladies in the shop, and justice demands that he should make it.

*　　*　　*

In conclusion, it is but justice to Mr. Cook to say that, whatever his faults may have been, the conduct of the parties [who] interviewed him was hasty, ungenerous, and unworthy of men whose long life in the community added to their mercantile integrity had won the respect of large circles of acquaintances. Had they withheld the information obtained from Mr. Cook, the proprietors of the shop referred to might never have known who was meant, and respectable, hard-working women would not have suffered from an uncalled-for notoriety, and the public might have failed to guess where the arrow hit. That both sides have said things which they would be glad to recall we have no doubt; and with all due respect for Mr. Bubier, we have no excuse for his extraordinary conduct on Sunday evening last, even though it be, as claimed, that his motive was to protect the character of the working people of Lynn. Believing that the favorable representations made to us in regard to the characters of the females employed in the shop mentioned are true, we think the Rev. Mr. Cook's duty is clearly defined, and that the circumstances of the case imperatively demand an apology from him to the ladies referred to.

We would caution the working men against the effects of heated

discussions on the subject, for discussions and differences in their ranks will lead to disastrous results. Remember the old motto:
"United, we stand,
Divided, we fall."
Lynn little Giant, February 4, 1871.

The Catholic Church regarding the Rev. Mr. Cook and the Reform Question

MR. EDITOR: I am led to notice this question of reform in the shops of this city from the agitation lately made about them. As pastor here of the Catholic Church for the last twenty years and upwards, I think I ought not to be silent on a question affecting the reputation of this city, and of the people under my charge.

I will venture to say that no person here knows so well the trials, the difficulties, and the troubles which are met with in families and in shops as I do. Besides, I have travelled considerably in this country, and have visited many cities and towns in England, Ireland and France, and I find here as much goodness, devotion and piety, and as few real evils, as I have found elsewhere; indeed, taking the population into consideration, I believe the evils here are less.

Now, so far as the Rev. Mr. Cook, who professes orthodoxy, advocates appropriate rooms or halls for girls and men to work apart, and that no communication should be held between each other during the hours of labor, and that competent women superintend the girls' department, and competent men the men's department, so far as practicable, I heartily concur with him; not because I condemn the present system, but that this separation would be more fitting, more conducive to good order, more beneficial for the public good, and more in harmony with Christian civilization. I am, then, in favor of a committee of one being appointed from each church, to meet, consult together, and attend to this matter. It is our duty as instructors, directors and guides of the people to guard against abuses, and see that the divine truths which religion teaches may be made known, so as to promote the good conduct and the spiritual welfare of all.

But so far as the Rev. Mr. Cook used language to convey the impression of the immorality of girls and men working in shops and halls, I am opposed to him. The names of girls and men have been brought before the public, and he is said to have alluded to them as a vile and degraded class, corrupt and corrupters. This charge he has not denied, for he says he has nothing to change. He adds that some halls there are, "some seventy feet in length by twenty in width, where the moral condition is bad, and the moral danger of the arrangements great,"—and thus the city is filled with these people, and filled with iniquity.

Now I say that this charge is a detraction and a calumny on the working girls and men of this city. The Rev. Mr. Cook makes it, and he sins grievously. Detraction is the unjust taking away of our neighbor's reputation, or the lessening of the good esteem in which he is held. This is done by giving publicity to faults hitherto secret. When the charge is false or the circumstances exaggerated it is a calumny. The Scriptures say, in Proverbs, chapter 24, verse 9, that the detractor or scorner is an abomination of men. And, in Ecclesiastes, chapter 10, verse 11, "The serpent will bite without enchantment, and a babbler is no better." Again, St. Paul, chapter 1, verses 30 and 32, says that backbiters, inventors of evil things, etc., are deserving of death. And again to the Corinthians, chapter 6, verse 10, "Neither drunkards nor revilers will inherit the kingdom of God."

Further testimony is unnecessary. Now the gravity of this sin is to be judged from the number of persons injured, from the damage they may suffer in their reputation, from the quality of the detractor, and from the number of persons who concur, or who may hereafter be led to concur, with him. Indeed, an evil report affecting the morality of a city is a diabolical sin, which tends to break up the peace of people and of families. In this case it is a sin against truth, charity, and justice. It displeases God, and tends to deceive men. It displeases God, who is the God of truth, and imitates the devil, who is the father of lies and of liars. It tends to deceive men by representing falsehood for truth.

I am told that Mr. S. M. Bubier, who has largely contributed to the prosperity of this city, being present on the occasion, manifested his disapprobation in unmeasured terms. He could not suffer the working-class to be abused, and the good name of this city to be arraigned, without raising his voice against it. Had he left the hall, it might have been sufficient to show his disapprobation; but, fired with indignation, he wished to stand up boldly and manfully, and rebuke the foul detraction from the very spot it sprung. Indeed, hardened must be the heart—I had almost said soulless must be the man—that would attack poor, honest, industrious, and defenceless girls, who wend their way on foot, by the dawn of the morning, amid the cold blasts of winter, to these shops and halls, and when the labors of the day are over, tired and weary, at the shades of the evening they return to perhaps comfortless homes. Thus they toil to earn an honest livelihood for their parents, for their little brothers, and for themselves.

I have now presented my views on this agitated question, and entertain no unfriendly feelings to Rev. Mr. Cook. Indeed, I wish him every success in his efforts to improve the people of his charge. Respectfully yours,

PATRICK STRAIN,
Pastor of St. Mary's Church

Lynn Semi-Weekly Reporter, February 11, 1871.

Appendix A

The old New England mill towns were greatly romanticized by contemporaries. For those looking back upon the process of antebellum industrialization such towns seemed like utopian communities, "machines in the garden," and models for the future. They became models at the very time that their reality had strayed farthest from the myth. In the early nineteenth century some Boston cotton merchants— troubled by restrictions on the overseas markets for raw cotton, owing to Anglo-American conflict, and eager to increase profits by adapting English textile mill techniques to the United States—invested in the Boston Associates, a massive limited-liability corporation which then built a totally integrated factory structure. To secure labor for the mills, the Boston Associates tried to construct supervised communities that would be acceptable to New England farm families, and that would enable the corporation to tap the surplus labor force of a declining agricultural region. The system, developed in Waltham and later applied on a massive scale in Lowell, proved not only profitable but exciting to the early-nineteenth-century observer. The supervised boarding houses and rural setting of the Lowell factory community was in vivid contrast to the harsh English textile communities of Lancastershire, as vividly described by such novelists as Elizabeth Gaskell. Hundreds of farm women were drawn to Lowell to labor in the mills for a time, usually two to seven years, before returning home or moving on. These young women (over 90 percent native-born) attended lectures and published a newspaper of poetry, fiction, and essays. Their youth, the rural setting, and the impressions conveyed in their newspaper convinced many observers that America had found an alternative to the harshly oppressive industrialization of the Old World. Profit and morality, at least in America, seemed to have found a happy balance.

Unfortunately, the reality of Lowell, Lawrence, and the other anti-bellum mill towns was not quite as utopian as initially suspected. Although in the early years Lowell managed to avoid the problems associated with industrialization, the mills were not all their protagonists claimed they were. Women, who occupied the unskilled jobs, were not found in supervisory positions, and their wages were less than half those of the male employees. The boardinghouses were crowded; the factories were hot, humid, and virtually airless; working hours were long—twelve to thirteen hours a day; rules and discipline were harsh and often arbitrary. And even these conditions began to deteriorate in the late 1830s. With increased competition from England and from expanding mills in New England, wages were cut and machines speeded up. In 1834, "Lowell girls" walked out to protest a 15 percent wage reduction; in 1836, there was another major strike against increases in the price of room and board. A distinctly nonutopian image emerged, as reflected in a protest song of the time, which went:

Oh! Isn't it a pity that such a pretty girl as I
Should be sent to the factory to pine away and die?
Oh! I cannot be a slave;
I will not be a slave,
For I'm so fond of liberty
That I cannot be a slave.[72]

The conditions which led to the strikes of the 1830s worsened with the depression of 1837 which, at the same time, killed this early strike activity. When the mills reopened in the 1840s Lowell women workers were not as independent as before. As the regional farms deteriorated, many now came to work permanently at the mills; they were joined by women and men with fewer options than the old "Lowell girls," particularly immigrants from the British Isles. Although many of these women still held tenaciously to the traditional rural image of the "Lowell girls," signs indicating increased dissatisfaction with the system had begun to emerge. In 1845, the Female Labor Reform Association was formed, and conditions were bad enough to bring national attention by the end of the decade. Lowell mills operatives were now sending massive petitions calling for a ten-hour day to the state, and the Female Labor Reform Association was pushing its case for an end to the slavery of the mill worker. By now, too, Lowell's new immigrant textile operatives were active in the strike campaign.

Despite all this activity the image of the peaceable, contented Lowell girls died slowly. It was an Arcadian image of industrialization that appealed to middle-class America, and its glowing residue remained. Hence, as Americans were looking to Lowell as a model for the future, the city's conditions were markedly deteriorating. Moreover, the mills of southern New England—which never attempted to present such utopian imagery—were rapidly outstripping those of the northern region based on the Lowell model. Fall River, particularly, which took a more Lancastershire approach to mill operations, had by the 1860s replaced Lowell and Lawrence as the major center for cotton textile production in the United States.

Notes

1. Joseph Cook, *Music Hall Lectures, Embracing Five Addresses on Factory Reform in the Largest Trade of the U.S.* (Boston: W. H. Halliday & Co., 1871), p. 16.

2. Quoted in R. Jackson Wilson, *In Quest of Community: Social Philosophy in the U.S., 1860–1920* (New York, Oxford Univ. Press, 1968), p. 39.

3. See Cook, *Music Hall Lectures*, p. 10.

4. See Appendix A.

5. See David Montgomery, *Beyond Equality* (New York: Random House, 1967), and *Historical Statistics of the United States* (Washington, D.C.: Bureau of Census, 1975).

6. *Eighth Census of the United States: Manufacturing, 1860* (Washington, D.C.: Bureau of Census, 1861).

7. Quoted in Thomas Cochran and William Miller, *A Social History of Industrial America* (New York: Harper and Row, 1961), p. 113.

8. David Johnson, *Sketches of Lynn or the Changes of Fifty Years* (Lynn: [no publisher given], 1880), pp. 11,20.

9. Ibid., p. 356.

10. Ibid., p. 22.

11. Ibid., p. 22

12. Thomas Cockran and William Miller, *A Social History of Industrial America*, p. 113.

13. See Joseph Cook for concern about the "floating population and the congregation of labor," in *Music Hall Lectures*, p. 14.

14. See Alan Dawley, *Class and Community: The Industrial Revolution in Lynn* (Cambridge: Harvard Univ. Press, 1976), p. 83.

15. See Alan Dawley, *Class and Community,* for a further discussion of the strike.

16. The transcendentalists were the main intellectual group in New England in the antebellum period. They believed that truth could be determined through individual action and that the moral person would act

according to his/her own moral principles, which could be determined through intuition. Emerson and Thoreau, probably the best known of the transcendentalists, had tremendous influence on the New England middle class.

17. See George Fredrickson, *The Inner Civil War: Northern Intellectuals and the Crisis of the Union* (New York: Harper and Row, 1965).

18. The letters between Joseph Cook and his parents have been collected and published by Frederick Bascom as *Letters of a Ticonderoga Farmer* (Ithaca: Cornell Univ. Press, 1946). Since the letters are arranged chronologically, and since their dates of composition are important to this study they will be cited, hereafter, as *Letters,* with their dates. *Letters;* Nov. 16, 1856.

19. *Letters,* April 6, 1856.

20. *Letters,* March 7, 1855, Oct. 19, 1859.

21. *Letters,* Nov. 24, 1855; June 21, 1857.

22. *Letters,* April 29, 1855.

23. *Letters,* May 27, 1855; June 18, 1855.

24. *Letters,* April 29, 1855.

25. Ibid. April 29, 1855.

26. *Letters,* June 18, 1855; Nov. 24, 1855; April 6, 1856.

27. See Steven Shapin, "Phrenological Knowledge and the Social Structure of Early 19th Century Edinburgh," *Annals of Science* 32 (1975): 219–243.

28. *Letters,* May 20, 1860; Sept. 16, 1860.

29. *Letters,* Sept. 16, 1860.

30. *Letters,* Jan. 30, 1859.

31. *Letters,* Jan. 20, 1861.

32. *Letters,* June 3, 1859.

33. *Letters,* Jan. 10, 1859; Dec. 31, 1858.

34. *American Journal of Insanity* 16, (1859), pp. 107, 108; Ibid. 17 (1860), p. 462. See also Barbara Rosenkrantz and Maris Vinovskis, "Sustaining the Flickering Flame of Life: Accountability and Culpability for Deaths in Ante-bellum Massachusetts' Asylums," in Susan Reverby and David Rosen, eds., *Health Care in America* (Philadelphia: Temple Univ. Press, 1979).

35. *Letters,* March 7, 1855; June 21, 1857.

36. Joseph Cook, *Transcendentalism* (Boston: J. R. Osgood & Co., 1877), pp. 9, 10.

37. Herbert Spencer, an English economist, argued in his work *Social Statistics,* which became extremely influential in this country, that society was like Darwin's biological evolutionary system—a struggle in which the fittest rose to the top.

38. Cook, *Music Hall Lectures,* p. 31.

39. Joseph Cook, *Socialism* (Boston:Houghton Mifflin, 1893 ed.), p. 40.

40. Cook, *Music Hall Lectures, pp. 4, 5.*

41. Ibid, p. 4.

42. *Letters,* June 10, 1872.
43. *Letters,* Aug. 18, 1872.
44. Cook, *Music Hall Lectures,* p. 9.
45. Ibid.; Cook, *Socialism,* p. 50; ibid., p. 156.
46. Cook, *Music Hall Lectures,* p. 33; [Add cite?]; Ibid., p. 34.
47. Ibid., p. 36.
48. Cook, *Socialism* pp.89, 44.
49. Ibid., p. 77.
50. Cook went on to argue that the poor were potentially dangerous in that, although they might be inferior, they nonetheless could turn themselves into an army. Cook argued next that the answer was not more military might, as Daniel Rodgers argued in *The Work Ethic in Industrial America, 1850–1920* (Chicago: Univ. of Chicago Press, 1978), but more public education and church work among the poor.
51. Cook, *Music Hall Lectures,* pp. 20, 19.
52. Ibid., p. 17.
53. Ibid., p. 81.
54. Ibid., pp. 81, 82, 30.
55. Ibid., p. 28.
56. It may be true that the Victorian image of womanhood was in conflict with not only working class women, but middle-class women as well.
57. Cook, *Music Hall Lectures,* p. 81.
58. Ironically, the middle class were much more the captains and the manufacturers the generals, as was seen in the continual backing down of the middle class to the manufacturers on such issues as police defense of scabs and use of outside force.
59. Cook, *Socialism,* pp. 89, 78, 88.
60. Ibid., p. 70.
61. Charles Hopkins, *The Rise of the Social Gospel in American Protestantism* (New Haven: Yale Univ. Press, 1940), p. 39. See also Authur Mann, *Yankee Reformers in the Urban Age* (Cambridge: Harvard Univ. Press, 1954) and Henry May, *Protestant Churches and Industrial America* (New York: Octagon Books, 1963) for a more extensive discussion of Cook and his role in social reform thought.
62. Although the concept of the dangerous nature of the lower classes and the possibility that environment was creating an inferior class was not central to late-nineteenth-century reform ideology, the message was not far below the surface of reform arguments. Indeed, Riis's image of the poor as oppressed but also dangerous was an important part of his message. He also argued in his most famous tract, *How the Other Half Lives,* (New York: Scribner, 1897), that the poor should be helped not only to prevent moral contragion, but also to counteract the specter of the "Man with the Knife." Even Jane Addams worried about the lower classes of immigrants which were filling up the cities.
63. Cook, *Music Hall Lectures,* pp. 139, 140.

64. Ibid., pp. 47–49.
65. Ibid., p. 75.
66. Ibid., pp. 45, 59, 60.
67. Ibid., p. 72.
68. *Semi Weekly Reports,* February 11, 1871.
69. Cook, *Music Hall Lectures,* p. 26.
70. *Semi Weekly Reports,* March 4, 1871.
71. Walter Rauschenbusch *Christianity and the Social Crisis,* (March, 1907).
72. Quoted in Philip Foner, *Women and the Labor Movement* (New York, Macmillan Co., 1979), p. 35.

Selective Bibliography

Joseph Cook managed not only to reach a large audience with his Boston and Lynn lectures, but he also published a series of lectures which are a useful source to his ideas about Darwinism, biology, heredity, and theology as well as industrial reform. See particularly his *Socialism* (Boston: Houghton Mifflin, 1893): *Transcendentalism* (Boston: J. R. Osgood, 1877); *Current Religious Perils* (Boston: Houghton Mifflin, 1888); *Biology* (Boston: J. R. Osgood, 1877); and *Music Hall Lectures* (Lynn, 1871). See also Alice Williams, ed., *Brilliants, Selected Writings of Joseph Cook* (New York: H. M. Caldwell, 1893); and Frederick Bascom, ed., *Letters of a Ticonderoga Farmer; Selections from the Correspondence of William A. Cook and His Wife with Their Son Joseph Cook, 1851–1885* (Ithaca: Cornell Univ. Press, 1946).

For a general description of the changing nature of the American economy, which affected the era Cook lived through, see Thomas Cochran and William Miller, *The Age of Enterprise* (New York: MacMillan Co., 1941); and David Montgomery, *Beyond Equality: Labor and the Radical Republicans 1862–1872* (New York: Random House, 1972); for a more general view see Sam Hays, *The Response to Industrialism, 1885–1914,* (Chicago: Univ. of Chicago Press, 1957). For a description of the response of the early social thinkers to this change, see George Fredrickson, *The Inner Civil War, Northern Intellectuals and the Crisis of the Union* (New York: Harper & Row, 1965); R. Jackson Wilson, *In Quest of Community: Social Philosophy in the United States 1860–1920* (New York: Oxford Univ. Press, 1968); and William L. Barney, *Flawed Victory: A New Perspective on the Civil War* (Washington, D.C.: University Press of America, 1975). For a more detailed discussion of the impact of industrial and urban change on social reform and the social gospel movement, see Cliford Clark, *Henry Ward Beecher, Spokesman for a Middle-Class American* (Urbana: Univ. of Ill. Press, 1978); Charles Hopkins, *The Rise of the Social Gospel in American Protestantism* (New Haven: Yale Univ. Press, 1940); Henry May, *Protestant Churches and Industrial America* (New York: Octagon Books, 1963); Aaron Abell, *The Urban Impact of American Protestantism, 1865–1900* (Cambridge: Harvard Univ. Press, 1943); Arthur Mann, *Yankee Reformers in the Urban Age* (Cambridge: Harvard Univ. Press, 1954); and Daniel Rodgers, *The Work Ethic in Industrial America, 1850–1920* (Chicago: Univ. of Chicago Press, 1978). Both Hopkins and Mann have extensive coverage on Cook in their works.

For a general discussion of social reform movements, see Robert Bremner, *From the Depths, The Discovery of Poverty in the United States* (New York: New York Univ. Press, 1956). Richard Hofstadter, *Social Darwinism in American Thought* (Boston: Beacon Press, 1955) has an excellent discussion of the impact of Darwin on American social thought. Allen Davis, *American Heroine, the Life and Legend of Jane Addams* (New York: Oxford Univ. Press, 1973) is a good portrayal of the social thought of Jane Addams, and her own *Twenty Years at Hull House* (New York: MacMillan, 1912) is still one of the best descriptions of the making of a late-nineteenth-century social reformer. For the views of a social reformer with many of the prejudices first articulated by Cook himself, see Jacob Riis, *How the Other Half Lives* (New York: 1957 ed.). Edward Bellamy's *Looking Backward* (Boston: Tickmor & Co., 1888) represents many of Cook's concerns put in a radical as opposed to a conservative framework. Oscar Handlin's *Boston's Immigrants* (Cambridge: Atheneum, 1959) is a nice background for anyone trying to understand the values that permeated Boston during the early period. For a general review of the literature and a discussion of social reform in industrial cities, see John Cumbler, "The Politics of Charity, Gender and Class in Late 19th Century Charity Policy," *Journal of Social History* (Sept., 1980): 99–111.

There have been several studies of the city of Lynn. The two most recent ones which deal with the Reverend Joseph Cook are, Alan Dawley, *Class and Community, The Industrial Revolution in Lynn* (Cambridge: Harvard Univ., 1976); and John Cumbler, *Working Class Community in Industrial America* (Westport: Greenwood Press, 1979).

Index